SSR Paper 23

Accountability, Discourse, and Service Provision: Civil Society's Roles in Security Sector Governance and Reform (SSG/R) and Sustainable Development Goal-16 (SDG-16)

Aries A. Arugay & Justin Keith A. Baquisal

ubiquity press
London

Published by
Ubiquity Press Ltd.
Unit 3N, 6 Osborn Street
London E1 6TD
www.ubiquitypress.com

DCAF – Geneva Centre for Security Sector Governance
Maison de la Paix, Chemin Eugène-Rigot 2E, P.O. Box 1360
CH-1211 Geneva 1, Switzerland
www.dcaf.ch

First published 2024

Cover photograph © United Nations Photo – Human Rights Council

Print and digital versions typeset by Siliconchips Services Ltd.

ISBN (Paperback): 978-1-914481-44-4
ISBN (PDF): 978-1-914481-45-1
ISBN (EPUB): 978-1-914481-46-8
ISBN (Mobi): 978-1-914481-47-5

Series: SSR Papers
ISSN (Print): 2571-9289
ISSN (Online): 2571-9297

DOI: https://doi.org/10.5334/bcy

The full text of this book has been peer-reviewed to ensure high academic standards.
For full review policies, see https://www.ubiquitypress.com/

Suggested citation:
Arugay, A. A. & Baquisal, J. K. A. 2024. *Accountability, Discourse, and Service Provision:
Civil Society's Roles in Security Sector Governance and Reform (SSG/R)
and Sustainable Development Goal-16 (SDG-16)*.
London: Ubiquity Press.
DOI: https://doi.org/10.5334/bcy. License: CC-BY-NC

To read the free, open access version of this book
online, visit https://doi.org/10.5334/bcy or scan
this QR code with your mobile device:

Abstract

Civil society has become an indispensable part of the global discourses on democratization, good governance, sustainable development, and security. Differing perspectives view civil society as a legitimizing actor, a critical partner, and even a serious challenger in these discourses. This paper examines the ways in which civil society actions contribute to Security Sector Governance and Reform (SSG/R) and Sustainable Development Goal-16 (SDG-16). It argues that civil society's ability to make significant contributions to SSG/R and SDG-16 rests on the interplay between endogenous factors such as its plurality, robustness, and civility, and exogenous variables such as the regime type, state capacity, and relations with security providers. The differing combinations of these factors enable civil society to perform three major roles as: (1) an agent of democratic accountability and civilian oversight; (2) a space for new discourses on security and development; and (3) an alternative provider of people-oriented security. This paper uses case studies of the Philippines, Tunisia, and Somalia, among others, to show the variation in the performance of these roles, the gains achieved by civil society organizations (CSOs), and the limitations and challenges posed by their involvement. It argues that the efforts of civil society to improve SSG help meet some of the targets of SDG-16 that relate to improving accountability, transparency, and participation. This paper concludes by examining the implications of civil society's participation in the future sustainability of SSG/R as a framework and the progress toward the realization of SDG-16 and providing viable policy recommendations for actors at the international, state, and societal levels.

Contents

Dedication   vii

SSR Papers   ix

About the Authors   xi

Declaration   xiii

Acknowledgments   xv

Executive Summary   xvii

List of Abbreviations   xix

I.   **Introduction**   1
     a. A roadmap   2
     b. Security sector governance and reform   2
     c. Sustainable development and SDG-16   3
     d. Civil society   4
     e. Roles of civil society in SSR/G and SDG-16   4
     f. Scope and methodology   6

II. **Civil Society at the Nexus of Security & Development: A Literature Review**   9
     a. Civil society: theoretical perspectives   10
     b. Principles and goals of SSG/R   12
        b.1. SSG/R and development   15
        b.2. SSG/R and democratization   17
        b.3. SSG/R and peacebuilding   18
        b.4. SSG/R, civil society, and local ownership   19
     c. Civil society and the principles and aims of SDG-16   21
     d. SSG/R, SDG–16, and civil society   25

III. **Analytical Framework: Civil Society as an Oversight Agent,
     Space for Discourse, and Alternative Security Provider**   29
     a. Civil society's endogenous and exogenous factors   29
     b. Three primary roles of CSOs in SSG/R   30
     c. Impact of civil society's SSG/R roles on SDG-16   32

IV. **Case Studies**   35
     a. Civil society in the Philippines: providing oversight and accountability   36
        a.1. Endogenous factors   36
        a.2. Exogenous factors   37

a.3. *CSO roles*   38

a.4. *Impact on SDG-16*   39

b. Civil society in Tunisia: toward becoming a space for security discourse   42

b.1. *Exogenous factors*   43

b.2. *Endogenous factors*   43

b.3. *CSO roles*   44

b.4. *Impact on SDG-16*   46

c. Civil society in Somalia: the pursuit of alternative security provision   48

c.1. *Exogenous factors*   49

c.2. *Endogenous factors*   50

c.3. *CSO roles*   51

c.4. *Impact on SDG-16*   52

V.   **Conclusions & Policy Recommendations**   55

a. Main findings   55

b. Policy recommendations   57

VI. **References**   61

Dedication

To Professor Emeritus Carolina G. Hernandez of the University of the Philippines-Diliman, a rigorous and prolific political scientist, a staunch advocate of security sector reform in Asia, and a credible public servant who pushed for more democratic civil-military relations in the Philippines.

SSR Papers

The DCAF SSR Papers provide original, innovative, and provocative analysis on the challenges of security sector governance and reform. Combining theoretical insight with detailed empirically driven explorations of state-of-the-art themes, SSR Papers bridge conceptual and pragmatic concerns. Authored, edited, and peer reviewed by SSR experts, the series provides a unique platform for in-depth discussion of a governance-driven reform agenda, addressing the overlapping interests of researchers, policy-makers, and practitioners in the fields of development, peace, and security.

DCAF – Geneva Centre for Security Sector Governance is dedicated to improving the security of states and their people within a framework of democratic governance, the rule of law, respect for human rights, and gender equality. Since its founding in 2000, DCAF has contributed to making peace and development more sustainable by assisting partner states, and international actors supporting these states, to improve the governance of their security sector through inclusive and participatory reforms. It creates innovative knowledge products, promotes norms and good practices, provides legal and policy advice, and supports capacity-building of both state and non-state security sector stakeholders.

About the Authors

Aries A. Arugay (Georgia State University, Ph.D.) is Professor and Chairperson at the Department of Political Science at the University of the Philippines Diliman. He is also Visiting Senior Fellow and Coordinator of the Philippine Studies Programme at the ISEAS – Yusof Ishak Institute (Singapore). His research interests are comparative democratization, security sector governance, foreign and security policy, and digital politics. Aries is the Editor-in-Chief of *Asian Politics & Policy*, a journal in political science and international relations published by Wiley-Blackwell and the Policy Studies Organization. He has published in *Asian Perspective, Pacific Affairs, Journal of East Asian Studies, American Behavioral Scientist*, and the *Journal of Current Southeast Asian Affairs*, among others.

Justin Keith Baquisal is a Resident National Security Analyst at FACTS Asia and a Southeast Asia Young Leader at the International Institute for Strategic Studies' Shangri-La Dialogue. He has a degree in political science (magna cum laude) from the University of the Philippines Diliman and is currently a graduate student in the same institution. He has published policy briefs, op-eds, and academic articles on Philippine national security, foreign policy, and autocratization, which have appeared in *Southeast Asian Affairs, Pacific Affairs, The Diplomat, Fulcrum*, and *Asialink*.

Declaration

Acknowledgments

We would like to thank the excellent people of DCAF—Gabriela Manea, William McDermott, Alexandra Preperier, and Richard Steyne—for their helpful comments and support. We are also grateful to the two anonymous reviewers who helped improve this paper. Finally, we are thankful for the encouragement of Hans Born from DCAF to write this paper.

Executive Summary

Civil society has become an indispensable part of the global discourses on democratization, good governance, sustainable development, and security. Differing perspectives view civil society as a legitimizing actor, a critical partner, and even a serious challenger in these discourses. This study examines the ways in which civil society actions contribute to Security Sector Governance and Reform (SSG/R) and Sustainable Development Goal-16 (SDG-16). Both are change-oriented paradigms that are linked by the centrality of human security in development planning by focusing on individual needs in economic, health, environmental, personal, community, and political spheres.

This study argues that civil society's ability to make significant contributions to SSG/R and SDG-16 rests on the interplay between endogenous factors such as its plurality, robustness,and civility, and exogenous variables such as the regime type, state capacity, and relations with security providers. There is no single factor that determines the success of civil society in promoting SSG/R, but these factors form the environment in which civil society could play an active role in influencing SSG/R initiatives. This study found that a robust, diverse, pluralistic, and democratic civil society has the potential to contribute to SSR/G. Moreover, democratic governance, a well-capacitated state, and cordial relations between civil society and security providers are elements of an external environment conducive to civil society involvement in SSG/R. This study posits that the extent to which these factors are present defines the ability of civil society to perform three major roles: (1) as an agent of democratic accountability and civilian oversight; (2) as a space for new discourses on security and development; and (3) as an alternative provider of people-oriented security. This paper uses case studies of the Philippines, Tunisia, and Somalia, among others, to show the variation in the performance of these roles, the gains achieved by civil society organizations (CSOs), and the limitations and challenges posed by their involvement. It argues that the efforts of civil society to improve SSG help meet some of the targets of SDG-16 that relate to improving accountability,transparency, and participation. In so far as SSG/R and the SDGs are both discourses that seek to decenter focus on the state and sovereign power, civil society has the legitimacy to contribute to SSR as well as to the fulfilment of the SDGs. Consequently, civil society expands the focus of security assistance in policymaking on development and aid by drawing attention to non-traditional concerns relating to structural rather than direct violence which threatens the survival, livelihood, and dignity of people.

This study concludes by examining the implications of civil society's participation in the future sustainability of SSG/R as a framework and progress toward the realization of SDG-16 and provides policy recommendations for actors at the international, state, and societal levels. It recommends that the security sector and SSG/R donors recognize the role of civil society in SSR processes, appreciate its diversity and dynamic composition, and understand the politicized environment of civil society advocacy. More broadly, it also recommends integrating SDGs in SSG/R planning and frameworks.

List of Abbreviations

African Union Mission in Somalia (AMISOM)
Anti-Money Laundering/Countering Terrorist Financing (AML-CTF)
Armed Forces of the Philippines (AFP)
Bantay Bayanihan (BB)
Bertelsmann Transformation Index (BTI)
Civil society organization (CSO)
Communist Party of the Philippines-New People's Army (CPP-NPA)
Counterterrorism / preventing and countering violent extremism (CT/PCVE)
DCAF – Geneva Center for Security Sector Governance (DCAF)
Development Assistance Committee (DAC)
Financial Action Task Force (FATF)
Internal Peace and Security Plan-Bayanihan (IPSP-*Bayanihan*)
Internal Security Operations (ISO)
Millennium Development Goals (MDGs)
National Constituent Assembly (NCA)
North Atlantic Treaty Organization (NATO)
Organization for Economic Cooperation and Development (OECD)
Organization for Security Cooperation in Europe (OSCE)
Security Sector Governance and Reform (SSG/R)
Security Sector Reform (SSR)
Sustainable Development Goals (SDGs)
Tunisian Confederation of Industry, Trade, and Handicrafts (UTICA)
Tunisian General Labor Union (UGTT)
Tunisian Human Rights League (LTDH)
United Kingdom (UK)
United Nations (UN)
United Nations Development Program (UNDP)
United Nations Security Council (UNSC)

CHAPTER I

Introduction

From its roots in political theory, the concept of civil society has become part of the mainstream discourses of democratization, good governance, sustainable development, and security. Civil society often refers to social organizations and other collective groups pursuing private means for public ends. Given the importance accorded by different political actors at the domestic and international levels to participation, multi-sectoral consultation, and popular empowerment, civil society has been recognized as a catalyst, partner, critic, and even challenger of various security and development paradigms. Civil society organizations (CSO) have been seen as critical partners of states in governance, alternative provider of services and public goods, and important intermediaries between states and societies at large (Carroll and Jarvis 2015).

Over the years, the governance-oriented roles accorded to civil society expanded beyond domestic borders, given an emergent transnational civil society. Networks of CSOs engaged with other actors in global politics such as international organizations, multilateral funding agencies, and non-governmental entities to jointly pursue mutually shared goals such as democratic governance, sustainable development, and human security. The rise of global civil society linked a mélange of social organizations of varying backgrounds and ideologies but sharing a similar vision, principles, and goals. Rather than easily identifiable actors, transnational civil society is a complex network of different entities that rapidly expands and evolves in the world of security and development advocacy, such as those collective entities in global climate change and human rights regimes (Keck and Sikkink 1998; Tarrow 2005).

Civil society engagement with other transnational actors in international politics has resulted in new thinking on how security could be better provided, as well as ways to ensure that development is inclusive, sustainable, and people-oriented (Krause & Jutersonke 2014). For example, civil society actors have made significant efforts to promote Security Sector Governance and Reform (SSG/R) and Sustainable Development Goal (SDG) 16 on 'peace, justice, and strong institutions',

How to cite this book chapter:
Arugay, A. A. & Baquisal, J. K. A. 2024. *Accountability, Discourse, and Service Provision: Civil Society's Roles in Security Sector Governance and Reform (SSG/R) and Sustainable Development Goal-16 (SDG-16).* Pp. 1–7. London: Ubiquity Press. DOI: https://doi.org/10.5334/bcy.a. License: CC-BY-NC

two important global projects that directly deal with the interface between security and development. This paper examines the agency of and roles played by civil society within these two reform and change paradigms.

a. A roadmap

This paper has five main sections. After the introductory section, the second chapter provides a literature review covering topics such as civil society, SSG/R, and SDG-16, and recent scholarship that links all three themes. The third chapter presents the analytical framework that comprises the exogenous and endogenous factors that determine the extent to which civil society could influence SSG/R and SDG-16, as well as the three roles performed by CSOs. This is followed by the fourth chapter which is the empirical backbone of this paper. It discusses the three case studies where civil society has performed the roles of being an agent of civilian oversight (Philippines), a site for security discourse (Tunisia), and an alternative provider of security (several fragile and conflict-affected states). This paper concludes by examining the implications of civil society's participation in the future sustainability of SSG/R as a framework and the progress toward the realization of SDG-16 and providing viable policy recommendations for actors at the international, state, and societal levels.

b. Security sector governance and reform

SSG/R is a relatively new addition to existing discourses on democracy, security, peace, and development. The increasing worldwide attention on the importance of institutions belonging to the security sector is due to the vital role that this sector plays in the provision of security for the state and its people, its capacity to support or thwart democratization processes, and its contribution in the pursuit of a lasting peace. Traditionally conceived as including only the armed forces, the concept of the security sector has expanded to include all those (whether statutory or not) that have an impact in the provision of (in) security in each country, such as the police, the intelligence services, paramilitary organizations, militias, and private armed groups, as well as civilian oversight institutions, judicial and penal agencies, and civil society (Hänggi, 2003). SSG/R departs from the traditional preoccupation of defending the state, as the new focus of security is now every human being in society (i.e., human security). As a part of the larger security sector, CSOs are primarily seen as actors who 'engage in research, debate, and advocacy among other activities, and may be critical or supportive of the security services and the government's security policy. Their interest in ensuring high standards of public and state security provision makes them an integral part of the security sector' (DCAF 2015: 5).[1]

Scholars have also observed that with the traditional understanding of security, it is often the state whose dysfunctionality or overt persecution of its own citizens is the cause of insecurity and violence (Ball and Brzoska 2002). In the broadest sense, SSR may pertain to a 'plethora of issues and activities related to the reform of the elements of the public sector charged with the provision of external and internal security' (Hänggi, 2004: 4). SSR seeks a comprehensive and simultaneous transformation of key institutions and groups for them to guarantee the physical security of the people, but in doing so to also respect democratic principles and human rights. One of the most authoritative definitions of SSR came from the Development Assistance Committee (DAC) of the

---

[1] For a brief discussion on civil society and SSR, see also DCAF, "Civil Society: Roles and Responsibilities in Good Security Sector Governance," *SSR Backgrounder*, 1 May 2019, https://www.dcaf.ch/civil-society-roles-and-responsibilities-good-security-sector-governance.

Organization for Economic Cooperation and Development (OECD) which defined it as increasing the country's 'ability to meet the range of security needs within their societies in a manner consistent with democratic norms and sound principles of governance, transparency and the rule of law' (OECD, 2005: 3). The UN Security Council (UNSC) through its President in 2007 stressed that 'reforming the security sector in post-conflict environments is critical to the consolidation of peace and stability, promoting poverty reduction, the rule of law and good governance' (p. 1) leading to Resolution 2151 in 2014, the first time SSR was included in a binding UNSC decision.

While SSR is a process toward a normative goal of effective and accountable security provision, SSG is the result of a successful process of SSR, as security is provided in accordance with the principles of good governance (namely accountability, transparency, rule of law, participation, responsiveness, effectiveness, and efficiency). Good SSG is crucial for broader development processes, as without it, peace and security may be compromised, and with it, the conditions necessary for sustainable development.[2] This paper understands good security sector governance as encompassing three key principles: (1) *Accountability*, which exists when 'there are clear expectations for security provision, and independent authorities oversee whether these expectations are met and impose sanctions if they are not met'; (2) *Transparency*, which refers to a state where 'information is freely available and accessible to those who will be affected by decisions and their implementation'; and (3) *Participation*, which ensures that 'all men and women of all backgrounds have the opportunity to participate in decision-making and service provision on a free, equitable and inclusive basis, either directly or through legitimate representative institutions' (DCAF 2015: 3).

c. Sustainable development and SDG-16

For the first part of the 21st century, the global development agenda was encapsulated under the Millennium Development Goals (MDGs)—eight globally agreed goals in critical areas of gender equality and empowerment of women, poverty alleviation, education, child and maternal health, environmental sustainability, reduction of communicable diseases, and cultivating a global development partnership. With the expiration of the MDGs, the UN defined the contours of the Post-2015 Development Agenda through participatory planning centered on consultations and expert panels across member-states and global civil society from 2012 to 2015. A total of seventeen SDGs were designed to build on the MDGs, adopting a more holistic approach to development by including its social, economic, and environmental components. The High-Level Panel on the Post-2015 Development Agenda recommended a specific line to 'build peace and effective, open, and accountable institutions for all,' recognizing that freedom from insecurity, conflict, and violence is a cross-cutting precursor to development (UN 2013: 1). Consequently, peace and good governance were put in the spotlight as an enabling and core element of the new development framework under the SDGs.

The implementation of the MDG framework was often hampered by insecurity, violence, and lack of the rule of law, mainly because of weak institutions (Dursun-Özkanca 2021). The SDGs seek to address this gap by highlighting the importance of 'key security, human rights and rule of law factors that form the basis for development' (UNSG 2013: 6).

SDG 16 on 'peace, justice, and strong institutions' covers peace, access to justice, and the creation of effective, accountable, and inclusive institutions for governance. Since 2015, the two implementation indicators for achieving these targets have revolved around strengthening national institutions to prevent violence and combat crime and terrorism, as well as the promotion and enforcement of non-discriminatory, inclusive laws and policies. Like SSG/R, SDG-16 emphasizes the need for effective *and* accountable institutions, with attention to the participation of civil

---

[2] The author is grateful to the reviewers for this insight.

society as the end-users and beneficiaries (Zamfir 2020). While there is no complete overlap between SSR principles and SDG-16 targets, this paper focuses on their convergence, namely: (1) Develop effective, accountable and transparent institutions at all levels (16.6); (2) Ensure responsive, inclusive, participatory and representative decision-making at all levels (16.7); and (3) Ensure public access to information and protect fundamental freedoms, in accordance with national legislation and international agreements (16.10) (UN 2013: 1).

d. Civil society

The paper adopts the following definition of civil society as:

> *all the different kinds of groups that people form around a shared interest or vision of public interest: for example, charities, philanthropic or advocacy associations, clubs, guilds, trade unions, professional organizations, business associations, community or residency groups, indigenous or ethnic interest groups, faith-based organizations, think tanks, NGOs and independent foundations* (DCAF 2019: 2).

There are three important elements present in any member of civil society: public interest, voluntary organization, and nonprofit motives. This means that organizations that claim to be part of civil society pursue goals that directly benefit the society at large, are autonomous from the state, and do not seek to derive economic gain from their activities (DCAF 2019). These organizations represent sectors within society, engage in political activities, resort to collective action such as protests to express collective demands against the state or other governmental entities, and cooperate with other political actors to pursue shared goals. This paper used this broader definition to capture a larger set of societal actors that engage SSG/R and SDG-16 across varying social, political, and economic contexts.

e. Roles of civil society in SSR/G and SDG-16

According to DCAF, civil society activities that promote SSG/R include the following: (1) awareness raising; (2) advocacy; (3) monitoring and public oversight; (4) fact-finding, research, and analysis; and (5) service provision (DCAF 2019). These functions help promote principles of good SSG by aiding existing SSR processes. These functions, in turn, could also help realize the targets of SDG-16.

This paper has several objectives. First, it provides a comprehensive review of the involvement and participation of civil society in global discourses on security and development through extant research on SSG/R and SDG-16. It examines recent and authoritative scholarly and policy literature to discuss the ways in which CSOs could help achieve the goals of these two reforms and change paradigms. The second objective is to identify the critical conditions and factors internal and external to civil society that shape their roles regarding SSG/R. This paper accomplishes this by using an analytical framework influenced by existing theories of civil society. Third, this paper seeks to empirically provide in-depth case studies of countries where civil society actors were able to promote SSG/R and by extension, SDG-16. Likewise, the analysis of case studies will also show the limitations of civil society's influence as well as the challenges it faces in contributing to the goals of these two discourses. Finally, this paper provides some policy recommendations for the enhancement of civil society participation in the pursuit of SSG/R and in turn, SDG-16 across several stakeholders such as international organizations, states, governments, and civil societies.

This paper examines the agency and influence of civil society within two paradigms that link security and development: SSG/R and SDG-16. It specifically asks:

- What are the factors that lead civil society to have a significant impact and influence on SSR processes?
- What are the roles played by civil society in promoting SSG/R?
- What are the consequences of civil society's promotion of SSG/R on the targets set by SDG-16?

This paper offers three main arguments. First, it argues that civil society's ability to make significant contributions to SSG/R and therefore SDG-16 rests on the interplay between its endogenous and exogenous factors. The former refers to the size, composition, and diversity of the civil society sphere. On the one hand, *endogenous* or internal factors conform to the structural and value-related aspects of civil society (Anheier 2013). If civil society is more robust, plural, and civil, it is expected to make stronger contributions to the pursuit of SSG/R goals leading to progress toward SDG-16. *Exogenous* factors on the other hand refer to variables that focus on the political context and relational spaces afforded to civil society to be able to carry out its work, such as the type of regime, state capacity, and civil society's relations with security providers. In states that are more democratized, well-capacitated, and open to societal participation, one could expect that CSOs are better able to further the goals of SSG/R and SDG-16. A more elaborate discussion that integrates the paper's other arguments will be discussed in the third chapter of this paper.

Second, the given internal makeup of a particular civil society as well as its external environment influences its ability to perform roles conducive to the objectives of SSG/R and SDG-16. Drawing from the perspective that viewed civil society as an actor, space, and site (Alagappa 2004), this paper proposes that it could potentially perform three major roles, being: (1) an *agent* of democratic accountability and civilian oversight; (2) a *space* for new discourses on security and development; and (3) an alternative *provider* of people-oriented security. These three roles manifest the actorness of civil society in the mutual pursuit of the aims of the two discourses of SSG/R and SDG-16.

This more nuanced approach allows an analysis of civil society as a complex set of diverse actors that engages security providers, formal oversight institutions, and international institutions, among others. It also provides an opportunity to recognize specific types of civil society actors beyond the usual groups such as highly professionalized NGOs, think tanks, and transnational networks. This is in keeping with the debates on civil society drawn from critical theories of governance that now recognize contradictions and dynamic interactions within the public sphere. Rather than be limited to the complementary roles often accorded to civil society in realizing security and development goals, this understanding recognizes the less palpable roles of civil society as a promoter of novel discourses and an alternative provider of more human-centric and accountable security. Thus, the paper's approach to expose other less mainstream roles of civil society opens new avenues for debate, instigates possible policy reforms, and even opens new possibilities for producing solutions for human security, a goal also shared by SSG/R.

Third, the various roles played by civil society in promoting SSG/R could have important consequences for the realization of SDG-16. Specifically, civil society's emphasis on *accountability, transparency,* and *participation* in SSG/R have a direct impact on particular SDG-16 targets, namely: (1) Develop effective, accountable and transparent institutions at all levels (16.6); (2) Ensure responsive, inclusive, participatory and representative decision-making at all levels

(16.7); and (3) Ensure public access to information and protect fundamental freedoms, in accordance with national legislation and international agreements (16.10).[3]

This paper will integrate these three main arguments into a coherent analytical framework in Chapter 3.

f. Scope and methodology

The scope of the paper is limited to scholarly and policy-relevant literature mainly on SSG/R. Though it will also discuss how civil society's efforts to pursue the aims of SSG/R could have an impact on SDG-16, this paper will not be able to cover all governance processes that are critical for sustainable development. Another limitation concerns the relationship between SSG/R and SDG-16. It could be theorized that there could be a reciprocal causal relationship between the two which means that SSG/R could affect SDG-16 and vice versa. However, given the limitations of the current body of literature so far, this paper will only focus on the impact of SSG/R on the realization of the targets set by SDG-16. Perhaps future research could further examine the extent to which fulfillment of all SDGs could facilitate SSG/R process around the world.

This paper will also utilize the empirical evidence and experiences of countries in the Global South who are normally the recipients of SSG/R-related international assistance. This is to emphasize the importance of unfavorable domestic contexts often faced by states where critical problems of security governance are present. This choice also adheres to the existing scholarly demand to further envisage SSG/R from the viewpoint and voices of societies where local ownership of SSG/R processes remains a challenge (Schroeder et al. 2014; Ansorg and Gordon 2019). Finally, it complements the existing body of literature that often takes the perspective of donors, international institutions, and powerful states (Ansorg 2017; Ebo 2007).

This paper's methodology has two interconnected components. The first is a documentary and literature review of important scholarly and policy-relevant scholarship on civil society, SSG/R, and SDGs in recent years. This review enabled the paper to produce an analytical framework that is appropriate to explain the variation in the roles played by civil society in promoting SSG/R. The second methodological component of this paper is the analysis of several case countries that highlight the various roles of civil society in SSG/R: as an agent of civilian oversight (Philippines), a site for security discourse (Tunisia), and an alternative provider of security (fragile and conflict-affected states such as Somalia). This paper uses different country case studies from the Global South to show the variation in the performance of these roles, the gains achieved by CSOs, and the limitations and challenges posed by their involvement. The logic of case selection is based on a purposive design as these countries illustrate how each role is performed by civil society. Apart from the purposive nature of case selection, there is also a useful variation in the countries' security and development context. The third case study focusing on the alternative security provision role of CSOs comprises not just one country but several conflict-torn countries in Africa. This is the most novel and unanticipated role observed by community organizations. By having means of violence, this might call into question the civil nature of these societal actors. As this is the first opportunity to analyze this emergent role, the paper is limited to discussing whether the provision of security could be a legitimate and acceptable role for CSOs.

---

[3] It could be argued that SSG/R could also promote other SDG-16 targets but this paper limits its scope to those targets where civil society could make a significant contribution to their achievement.

Table 1: Case Studies.[4]

	Philippines	Tunisia	Somalia
Civil Society Freedom (2021)	Repressed	Obstructed	Repressed
Defense Sector Corruption Risk (2020)	Moderate	High	N/A
SDG Progress (2022) Score Rank	66.64 (95/163)	70.69 (69/163)	45.57 (160/163)

As seen from Table 1, there are differences across the selected case studies concerning some empirical indicators of security and development. For example, the extent of civic space critical for civil society varies from 'repressed' in the Philippines and Somalia (as an example of fragile and conflict-affected states) in 2021 to 'obstructed' in Tunisia. On the other hand, Tunisia in 2020 had a higher risk of corruption in the defense sector compared to the Philippines. In measuring progress toward meeting SDG targets in 2022, there is also variation across the three countries with Tunisia ranking 69th, while the Philippines belonged to the bottom half of the countries (95/163), and Somalia almost at the bottom of the SDG rankings. These differences are important in comparative analysis since they refer to the endogenous and exogenous factors this paper identified earlier.

This paper extensively uses secondary data sources such as extant scholarly work, policy papers, and government documents that are publicly accessible. While the paper benefitted from the author's own in-depth research on SSG/R in the Philippines, it mainly relied on secondary and online sources of information for the other sets of cases.

---

[4] Data collected by the author using various sources such as CIVICUS (https://monitor.civicus.org/), Transparency International's Government Defense Integrity Index (https://ti-defence.org/gdi/), and the UN Sustainable Development Report (https://www.un.org/sustainabledevelopment/progress-report/).

CHAPTER II

Civil Society at the Nexus of Security & Development: A Literature Review

This chapter reviews the relevant academic and policy-oriented literature on civil society, particularly its engagements in security and development discourses such as SSG/R and SDGs. It is divided into four sections. The first section summarizes the extant scholarship on major theories of civil society and its link with democratic governance, a critical assumption for successful civil society advocacy and participation in reform processes. The second section discusses the principles and evolution of the SSG/R paradigm. It focuses on how as a reform or change paradigm, SSG/R has made strides in fostering development, democratization, and peacebuilding through an approach that emphasizes local ownership. The third section reviews the literature on SDGs, while the concluding part of this chapter covers some of the recent literature that links civil society with SSG/R and SDG-16.

There is broad consensus around the statement that development and security are mutually reinforcing conditions for human progress. Countries that lack the rule of law and are mired in violence, and are predatory or weak states, also tend to be sites for violent political contestation that prevent or inhibit economic growth. Conversely, underdevelopment is a strong catalyst for the socioeconomic grievances that fuel armed conflict and insecurity (Zamfir 2020). The Institute for Economics and Peace argues that higher levels of violence drive down economic development by reducing investments and destabilizing the broader macroeconomic environment, which in turn also have downstream consequences for critical facets of human development such as life expectancy, poverty, and a whole gamut of quality-of-life indicators (Institute for Economic and Peace 2016).

The end of the Cold War left the development sector with pressing problems relating to fragile states—those experiencing systemic civil unrest and barely functional state institutions—and

---

How to cite this book chapter:
Arugay, A. A. & Baquisal, J. K. A. 2024. *Accountability, Discourse, and Service Provision: Civil Society's Roles in Security Sector Governance and Reform (SSG/R) and Sustainable Development Goal-16 (SDG-16).* Pp. 9–27. London: Ubiquity Press. DOI: https://doi.org/10.5334/bcy.b. License: CC-BY-NC

tyrannical ones, particularly in many 'third-wave' democracies that were concerned not only with immediate stabilization, but also post-authoritarian transition and democratic consolidation. On the one hand, there was global attention for security and its efficient provision. On the other hand, many development theorists and practitioners also looked at the first-order questions of justice and morals because state security forces also tend to be the source of insecurity when they routinely violate rights of citizens and are not accountable for such abuses (Detzner 2017).

The security sector—the military, police, courts, and other security apparatuses of the state—is an inescapable partner in development programming (Chanaa 2002). A legitimate monopoly of violence is a defining feature of the state; the security sector cannot be completely discarded unlike some authoritarian legacy institutions such as ruling political parties, nor can its governance be sidestepped given its fundamental importance as a precondition and structural enabler for development. The peace upon which development can be built thus needs to explicitly and immediately address crosscutting issues of public empowerment and inclusion, governmental transparency and accountability, and rights protection together with usual concerns for operational capability.

a. Civil society: theoretical perspectives

The concept of civil society has a long tradition in political theory. Discussions about the origins of civil society emanate from the works of various seminal political philosophers such as Locke, Adam Smith, Marx, Hegel, and Gramsci (Keane 1998). The concept received its widest recognition from the liberal tradition of democratic theory. Civil society as being based on the idea of bonds of trust and goodwill akin to social capital (Smith), the common will (Rousseau), and as a countervailing power that limits the state (Locke) became the dominant interpretation.

Modern theories emphasized the inexorable link between civil society and democracy. However, this did not come immediately as theories of democracy were fixated with elections as the *essence* of democracy. With the revival of social protest and political turbulence in the 1960s, there was a renewed interest in its democratic potential. According to Grugel, the study of the reemergence of social activism was placed in the perspective of civil society both intellectually and politically. It became a popular term to encompass the organizations and movements that directly or indirectly support, promote, or struggle for democracy and democratization (Grugel 2003). This led to the revival of interest in the ideas of French political philosopher Alexis de Tocqueville. In his *Democracy in America*, he argued that in democratizing societies, associations might serve as the functional equivalents of estates in absolutist societies, insofar as they contain and moderate state tyranny. They do so in the following ways. First, associations might serve representative functions with respect to the state. Second, associations develop capacities that support democracy. Third, they may serve as alternative forms of governance, so much so that they carry out tasks that would otherwise fall to the state (de Tocqueville 1969; Gellner 1994). This paper underscores these philosophical ideas from de Tocqueville since they are the foundations for our contemporary expectations of civil society as sources of accountability, capacity-building, and even service delivery.

Another catalyst to the revival of civil society has been the wave of transition of some 30 or more countries away from authoritarian rule from 1979 until 1992. This 'wave of democratization', stemming from the crises which befell authoritarian states, was largely propelled by civil society (O'Donnell et al. 1986; Huntington 1993). These dramatic episodes of civil society mobilization evoked the romance, excitement, and heady possibilities of democracy's third wave more than the image of civil societies mobilizing peacefully to resist, discredit, and ultimately overturn authoritarian rule. Similar waves of civil society-led political change were also seen in the post-communist revolutions in Europe, colored uprisings in central Asia, and the Arab Spring (McFaul 2002; Laverty 2008; Moghadam 2013).

The ability of civil societies to check state power, complement its governance functions, and evoke popular empowerment and participation made civil society an attractive idea to discourses focusing on democratization, good governance, and sustainable development. It eventually became the 'darling of donors' as well as an imperative to include in decision-making at the domestic and international arena (Carothers and Ottaway 2000; Kaldor 2003). The consensus seemed to be that putting civil society into most political processes is generally a good idea.

Civil society's contributions to democratic accountability also transcended state borders with the rise of global civil society. Global institutions such as the UN and the World Bank, and regional organizations such as the European Union, were quick to accept that civil society inputs can in some instances increase global governance accountability to disadvantaged and marginalized circles, including countries of the global south, impoverished people, women, and other social groups that experience silencing and exclusion (Scholte 2011). But at the same time, many scholars admit that there are limitations to the extent to which civil society can contribute to democratic goals such as accountability and representation. For example, access to these global actors is difficult, CSOs might not be equipped to engage these actors in terms of highly technical language and knowledge requirements, and civil society might not even be unified to mount a coherent collective strategy, that could result in unintended consequences detrimental to democratic accountability (Lang 2012).

Aside from the liberal tradition, theorizing on civil society also received significant attention from critical theory that espouses a more radical perspective. Basically, it criticizes the assumption that civil society is automatically inclusive, given the unequal distribution of resources that shape the contours of civil society itself. Moreover, while liberal theories view civil society basically as a facilitator to reduce the burden of governance, a mechanism to release tension between competing interests, and as a check on state power, this critical approach takes the view that civil society could transform the state and could be an instrument that could correct the imbalances of the state. For example, Cohen and Arato suggested that civil society has the dual function of offering a vision of a more participatory system and engaging in the public sphere to promote change (Baker 2003).

This plural and dynamic diversity of civil society that represents different orientations, ideologies, and even visions conform to an alternative theoretical view of civil society inspired by neo-Marxist thinker Antonio Gramsci. He believed that civil society is more an arena of contending social groups where a hegemonic bloc emerges, often carrying out the dominant ideology at a certain juncture. This 'healthy' contestation within the disparate social groups within civil society allows differences to challenge existing orthodoxies (Edwards 2009).

At the same time, a civil society that is ontologically an arena for competing discourses, rather than an actor, means there is no automatic relationship between civil society and reformism. This view holds that constituent concepts such as respect for rule of law, civility, and inclusivity are not inherent in civil society, and greatly varies depending on the groups struggling for dominance. What is important in this view is the voluntary pursuit of collective interests by organizations distinct from the state (White 2004). This conceptualization focuses less on the actual goals and behavioral dispositions of civil society, which are treated as variables rather than givens.

There was increasing attraction to alternative perspectives given the hegemonic view of civil society derived from the liberal tradition. One critique is the instrumentalist view accorded by liberals to civil society as a legitimizing agent of the state. According to democratic theorists, civil society's legitimization is only valid if the state itself is viewed as a legitimate power by society. This might be assumed in Western societies but is highly problematic in the Global South. Thus, the statist bias in the liberal tradition obfuscates the power of civil society. This critique was further extended with the rise of global civil society, as the international arena is not necessarily just a state writ large, given the absence of a world government (Cohen and Arato 1992).

A second critique of the radical perspective is the delimiting nature of the liberal tradition to identify acceptable forms of civil society to ones that are acceptable to the democratic state. The rise of the 'uncivil society' literature points to this bias, especially for more militant CSOs such as social movements, as they are supposed to undergo a process of demobilization after 'transition' and for the routinization of politics in the state (Rumford 2001). Putting qualifications of appropriateness onto civil society not only diminishes its plurality and diversity, but also calls into question the democratic credentials of a state that is supposed to be committed to democracy (Bernhard and Branco 2017).

This paper benefits from both liberal and radical or critical perspectives on civil society, as it expands the repertoire of understanding beyond the typical notion that civil society is a political actor that plays secondary roles to states and international institutions. As this paper also envisions civil society as a space for discourses, it is necessary to recognize the power of civil society for reflexivity.

When it comes to critical competence in discursive contests in the world system, civil society actors have one important advantage over states and corporations, which is their greater freedom to act on a reflexive basis. Reflexivity here means the ability to contemplate the constellation of discourses operative on a particular issue and to figure out how any action will affect that constellation. States are heavily constrained by their imperatives to ensure their own security, maintain legitimacy in the eyes of their own populations, and maximize economic growth (Dryzek 2012: 115).

This section provided a brief historical overview of civil society from the political science literature, particularly tapping into research in democratization and global governance. To recap, it observed the dominance of liberal theories that see civil society as an actor that limits the power of states and intergovernmental organizations as well as providing legitimacy to decision-making processes. However, mainly relying on such an approach prevents the recognition of the power asymmetry between states and civil societies, the neglect of the diversity of civil society and the struggles within this sphere of social action, and the reflexive ability of civil society to reimagine democracy, accountability, and representation as espoused by critical or radical theories. Thus, this paper utilizes the mainstream liberal approach as well as the alternative radical view of civil society in its analysis of how CSOs could influence SSG/R processes and in turn, meet the targets of SDG-16.

b. Principles and goals of SSG/R

SSG pertains to the application of good governance in the management, provision, and oversight of a state's security sector with the view of imbibing principles of accountability, transparency, gender equality, rule of law, public participation, and responsiveness as well as conventional requirements for effectiveness and efficiency. This stems from an understanding that in illiberal or non-democratic contexts, the security and justice sectors—due to issues such as impunity, lack of professionalism, and politicization—may themselves be the sources of conflict, violence, and everyday insecurity for citizens. Meanwhile, SSR is the way by which good SSG could be achieved by targeting parts of or the entirety of the security sector (e.g., the justice system, police, military, intelligence) through a process of political and technical reforms, whereby actors and institutions are made to operate in a manner consistent with democratic norms and good governance principles, to reduce the overall risk of conflict, improve human security, and lead to a secure environment that fosters sustainable development (OECD 2005; Ansorg and Gordon 2019). SSR is a multi-sectoral endeavor that involves state and non-state actors and covers a wide range of activities including legislation, policymaking, information and education campaigns, capacity-building, and training to ensure that a country's security sector is managed within a framework of democratic civilian control, human rights adherence, and rule of law.

According to Sedra (2010), the innovation of SSR over conventional security assistance is its theoretical fidelity to good governance or standards by which the security sector is held to account. This means that there is a shift away from the mere provision of material resources and other capability requirements of security forces, and a concerted effort toward reforms related to the management, monitoring, and mechanisms of accountability by security actors. Burt adds that this ideal set SSR apart from conventional security assistance during the Cold War (Burt 2016). The implementation of SSR has traditionally been strongest in the context of democratization where the conceptual focus is not merely on *creating* institutions that can provide security for citizens—as even many authoritarian regimes already have the basic capabilities—but to ensure that these state institutions *operate* according to liberal-democratic standards. In effect, SSR is closely wedded to the broader state-building agenda because it stitches together state power with the need for legitimacy and endorses norms of what forms of state behavior are acceptable and not acceptable.

At a programmatic level, SSR can be summed up in terms of objectives, areas of concerns, and dimensions of reform listed in Table 2 below.

Table 2: Objectives, Areas of Concern, Dimensions, and Approaches to SSR.

Objective	Area of Concern	Dimension	Approach
1. Establishment of effective governance, accountability, and oversight structures in the security system 2. Improved delivery of security and justice services 3. Development of local leadership and ownership of the reform process 4. Sustainability of justice and security service delivery	**Control:** civilian and democratic control over instruments of lethal force, adherence to rule of law, transparency, and financial management, building capacity to scrutinize defense policy and building an epistemic community for defense, training forces with requirements of democratic society in mind. **Capacity:** development of professional security forces and institutions able to carry out functions in an effective, efficient, and legitimate manner. **Cooperation:** reorienting organizations and promoting confidence and collaboration vertically (checks and balance) and horizontally within the state, and in collaboration with civil society, international development partners, and other stakeholders.	**Political:** promotion of civilian oversight (state and civil society) over the security sector and a healthy state of civil-military relations whereby security policies, priorities, and actions are made in accordance with legitimate and legal authority. **Economic:** efficient allocation of appropriate human, financial, and material resources. **Social:** achievement of outcomes in terms of security in life and property of citizens. **Institutional:** organizational elements of reform relating to the structure of security forces, functional differentiation, and definition of tasks, among others.	**Orthodox:** comprehensive reform across the entire security sector involving majority of areas of concern and dimensions of reform around all orthodox SSR objectives, with the medium- to long-term goal of building a liberal-democratic security sector. **Stabilization:** provision of a strategic breathing room in a country. Involves basic security, suppression of spoilers, and engagement of locals to undertake SSR. Mostly revolves around establishment of civilian oversight, transitional security forces, and dialogue and sensitization programs. **Train and Build:** focus on provision of capability-oriented security assistance without emphasis or urgency on accountability and governance aspects of the SSR package. Some degree of norm-institutionalization is embedded in training programs, but not as part of the overall strategic effort. Most associated with individual SSR projects.

Source: Author's framework, with elements adopted from Wulf (2011) and Detzner (2017).

SSG/R aims for both efficiency and procedural compliance to democratic oversight, as well as local ownership of the reform process to ensure it is sustained and delivered. As a derivative of this, SSR's goals can be divided into four categories. Firstly, civilian control over state institutions and actors to ensure democratic accountability is the defining normative standard of SSR, and thus the strategic goal of relevant programs. Secondly, SSR programs seek to improve the delivery of security and justice services, and introduce ancillary principles such as inclusiveness, access, and responsiveness in the performance of these functions. Thirdly, SSR also fosters local champions within the state and within civil society and maximizes local ownership of the reform process. Finally, in doing the above-mentioned goals, SSR also makes justice and security reform sustainable.

These four goals are typically achieved in three programmatic areas or lines of effort, which focus on the democratic *control* and oversight of security institutions, *capacitation*—or the development of professional security forces that carry out functions in an efficient, effective, and legitimate manner—, and institutionalizing platforms and policies for *collaboration* and inclusive governance. The 'theory of change' inherent in SSR is to build an effective and accountable security sector revolving around capacity development of security forces, the inclusion of and engagement of stakeholders in dialogues and decision-making, and the reform of security sector attitudes, behavior, and systems (Chikwanha 2021).

These goals are wide-ranging and tackle a broad range of politically sensitive issues such as a country's intelligence services, parliamentary oversight over security actors, judicial and penal reform, and even doctrinal matters relating to operating procedures of security forces. Consequently, these reforms are undertaken across multiple dimensions, including in the political, economic, social, and institutional domains. For instance, the restructuring of organizational elements within the security sector in the context of democratization also historically coincided with economic structural adjustment, where economic liberalization brought forth serious discussions about maintaining fiscal balance between 'guns and butter'—money spent on security is one tax dollar less for other development initiatives.

First, the conventional approach refers to the extent and way by which a country undertakes the mix of objectives, areas of concerns, and diversity in policy tools to cover various reform dimensions. Orthodox SSR, which some have noted to be the 'first generation SSR,' refers to conventional SSR that focuses on the normative agenda of good governance, rule of law, human rights protection, and civilian control, as reflected in key documents such as the Council of Europe's Parliamentary Assembly Recommendation 1713 in 2005, the OECD DAC Guidelines, and the 2008 UN Secretary-General's report on the role of the UN in SSR.

The second approach is a stabilization approach—often in fragile environments—where external actors come to directly provide security themselves to provide the local authorities with strategic breathing room. In this approach, SSR is more attuned to long-term local capacitation and engagement to provide basic security, suppress spoilers, and sustain stakeholder interest. Aspects such as democratization and oversight come much later since unlike orthodox SSR, stabilization requires much more than reorienting security forces to conform to constitutional and internal standards of legality, transparency, and accountability, but creating them in places where they do not exist or are not functional.

A third approach is what is described as the 'train and build approach' which focuses on capability-oriented security assistance, which has been criticized for subordinating the democratic and rights-promoting aspects of SSR and instead underscoring only those related to technical exercises, training, and acquisitions of equipment. This third approach arguably does not meet SSR as a concept, although many studies have observed that there has been a tendency to put together uncoordinated and otherwise traditional security programs as part of an otherwise nonexistent SSR agenda at the country level (Sedra 2010). Other studies have pointed to the fact that states that insist on national sovereignty 'pick and choose' only the technical components of SSR because these capacity-oriented reforms are relatively uncontroversial and do not necessarily disturb local power relations, unlike normative commitments to human rights, for example. As such, there is a tendency to go back to a train and build approach because democratic norms and state-society relations are harder to configure than the training and capacity-building of security and justice institutions.

The literature on how SSR is *practiced* generally observes that SSR has 'rarely been implemented in its comprehensive form' (Jackson 2018: 2). Consequently, this means that there is a need to analyze the broader approach taken by authorities in a country, based on how they implement their respective SSR program with respect to what dimensions, goals, and areas of concern are prioritized. Some have pointed out that SSG/R programming tended to privilege the technical nature of capacity-building of state security and justice agencies—which tended to dilute SSG/R as a form of traditional security assistance, bereft of the normative aspects that made it significant to begin with (Jackson 2018). This was due to a host of factors such as the short time-frame of donors that needed quick fixes, the huge financial cost of implementing comprehensive SSR, the unpalatability of SSR to entrenched elite interests in countries where democratization or liberalization were at the early stages, or even the very difficult task of implementing SSR goals in countries transitioning from authoritarian to democratic rule, wherein success would depend not just on SSR as a framework but on how local actors finessed its execution even against possible spoilers (Detzner 2017).

There have been calls for a second generation of SSG/R to be 'context-appropriate, locally rooted, flexible and long-term approaches that could transform the governance of security institutions and change state-society relations' (Baranyi 2019: 2). Sedra wrote that 'contemporary reform contexts are just too messy and volatile to neatly apply normative frameworks. The problem is that attempting to do so in a clumsy and overbearing fashion can provoke a backlash among local actors, and not only set back reform processes, but do harm, something we have seen time and time again' (Sedra 2010). At the policy level, this has split practitioners between those who call for boldness and more rigorous implementation of SSR's transformative liberal-democratic elements, while others who support a post-liberal approach present the case for caution and pragmatism as to the implementation of mainstream principles (Jackson 2018).

Several reports under DCAF have attempted to unpack how to bridge the gap between theory and practice, by looking at different approaches under hybrid second-generation SSR which still retains many of the features of first-generation approaches but have expanded to also include non-state actors, traditional judicial and security mechanisms, and the long-term process of change (Piché 2017; Bangura 2017). Others observe, however, that by and large, second-generation SSR remains state-centric, capacity-oriented, and non-transformative (Sedra 2010).

b.1. SSG/R and development

The conceptual shift from traditional security assistance to SSG/R and from economic development to sustainable and human development is undergirded by the problematization of what and for whom the nature of security and development is. In development studies and practice, there was a marked transition away from growth, economism, and output measurements toward the appreciation of the need for quality of life and richness of human experience. In contemporary development literature, the concept of human development was eventually replaced by 'sustainable development' given the understanding that environmental and temporal factors are also at play, aside from human and economic factors, in trying to meet needs of present and future generations. Sustainable development essentially broadened the understanding of development from economistic and state-centric concepts such as Gross Domestic Product or Per Capita

Income toward multidimensional individual and systemic levels of well-being. This reorientation also occurred in the security and justice sectors, which had seen a paradigm shift; where there had been a prioritization of territorial integrity, political stability, and security forces' efficacy in state-centered constructs of security, human security put the concerns of ordinary people in the limelight and the tangible effects of security on their daily lives. This brought attention to security issues that emanate from the state and its shortcomings, such as underdevelopment, unlawful detention, lack of civilian protection, and so on (Wulf 2011).

Some attribute the emergence of SSR as a brainchild of the development donors that realized it was difficult to implement development assistance efficiently and effectively in conflict-torn societies or worse, fragile states, because vertical and horizontal forms of violence seriously derail human development. Between the 1960s and 1980s, designers of development policy realized that it was faulty to assume that economic development would lead to peace in the Global South, which was then beset primarily by the twin problems of underdevelopment and political instability that led to civil strife and violent political changes. The security sector, if 'factionalized, wrong-sized, dictatorial, [and] non-professional' may itself be the source of insecurity and the tool of national elites to plunder, control, and coerce society to serve vested interests; at the same time, the security sector is the inescapable partner that must be reformed to establish peace (Chanaa 2002). As a concept, SSR has its roots in efforts by developed Western countries in the 1990s to consolidate the link between security and transitional and post-conflict development, through program-based interventions specifically targeting the management, oversight, and operation of security and justice institutions. The overall role of SSR is to provide an enabling and mutually constitutive environment within which sustainable development can take place (OECD 2005).

As a program, SSR can rightfully be characterized as 'donor-driven' in that the many European countries provided the impetus and resources for its adoption worldwide. The United Kingdom, for example, has helped shape the development of strategic thought and donor frameworks through the Global Conflict Prevention Tool and its programs for conflict-affected countries, shaping much of SSR thinking (Ball in Sedra 2010). In addition to this, SSR is not merely a value-neutral technical assistance or development program, but one that is laden with a decidedly liberal disposition and interest as to how security and justice sectors ought to be managed; undoubtedly, the normative requirements of SSR as a framework are tied to the development experience of the West, hence the emphasis on parliamentary oversight, human rights, and inclusivity, among others. Some scholars and practitioners have cautioned against this imposing tendency of donor agencies of developed countries and international organizations (Wulf 2011). At a more conceptual level, Ejdus (2018) argues that liberal-leaning interventionist development policies at the end of the Cold War reflected the civilizing mission ethos of the West to engineer liberal transformation elsewhere in the world, believing that structural adjustments designed to mimic its institutions would lead to the same outcomes. At the same time, it has been pointed out that the willingness of state and non-state actors in the Global South to partner with international donors for SSR indicates strong local interest in concepts of transparency, accountability, and inclusiveness as part of the broader goal to meld security with justice (Ball in Sedra 2010).

It must also be stressed that it is the poor and other marginalized groups (e.g., women and children) that are often the victims of an ineffective, unaccountable, and abusive security sector. If not by the security apparatus of government, these 'vulnerable' groups are susceptible to violence and insecurity perpetrated by non-statutory forces such as gangs, criminal syndicates, and private militias. The unbroken cycle of violence precludes individuals from benefitting from broader development processes and predisposes them to resort to violence to pursue their interests.

SSR also is associated with development as it ensures that the resources given to the security sector are in proportion to the security conditions of the country. Through 'right-sizing' the security sector, any excess in the resources could be transferred in implementing the other tasks of government such as the provision of socioeconomic services and poverty reduction programs.

b.2. SSG/R and democratization

Traditionally, security and democracy do not go together. As reflected in the debates found in political philosophy, freedoms or rights associated with democracy are often sacrificed at the altar of the state's defense of civil peace. To a great extent, the hallmark of security institutions such as the military has been its lack of transparency and openness to input from other actors. Though a public good, security has always been a policy area where there has been limited participation from other actors.

The then United Nations Secretary-General Kofi Annan highlighted the linkage between SSR and democratic governance when he noted that the security sector 'should be subject to the same standards of efficiency, equity, and accountability as any other service' (Hänggi 2004: 9). It is also acknowledged that a democratically run and accountable, effective, and efficient security sector is vital in promoting political stability. It has been recognized that the armed forces by nature are the ultimate expression of the important role of coercion in governance (Alagappa 2001). The absence or lack of democratic civilian control and professionalism constitutes a serious challenge for most consolidating democracies. In the end, the successful implementation of SSR could quell any threats to the democratic order and help ensure that democracy will be 'the only game in town.'

As mentioned in the previous sections, SSR's conceptual anchor is democratization and good governance; SSR is not merely about post-conflict stabilization but is a large component of the broader political transition of a country away from authoritarian rule. An unaccountable security sector is itself a risk to democratic reform, which is why SSR forms part of the reconfiguration of civil-military and state-society relations (Ginifer 2006). SSR has been a framework to engage and coordinate defense and democratic reforms in post-communist Europe (Hänggi 2004). The most illustrative case of how SSR is linked with democratization has been the conditions demanded by regional organizations such as the Organization for Security Cooperation in Europe (OSCE), National Atlantic Treaty Organization (NATO), the European Union (EU), and the Council of Europe of countries that are seeking membership. As part of their 'new defense diplomacy,' they have made programs and initiatives associated with SSR as strict criteria for post-communist countries to qualify for membership. These requirements consist of imposing democratic civilian control to include the judiciary, police, and parliament.

From the experience of democratizing societies, it is no guarantee that security will improve in the post-authoritarian period. On the contrary, it has been observed that authoritarianism's propensity to use repression has swept all unresolved issues 'under the rug' such that most democratic transitions have always featured episodes of armed conflict. Furthermore, Luckham also argued that the rude awakenings from the failure to meet expectations and demands in the post-transition period also could stoke political violence (Luckham 2003).

From the perspective of good governance, the security sector comprises a substantial portion of any government which often has tremendous resource endowments. Thus, the potential for any misallocation could be a great source of poor governance or malgovernance (Fitz-Gerald 2003). Even if one assumes that a country's security sector is democratically governed and lacks the propensity to seize state power, SSR also is important in socializing civilian politicians not to make any attempts to draw the armed forces, for example, to partisan politics and disrupt democratic processes (Edmunds 2004).

b.3. SSG/R and peacebuilding

Perhaps the more relevant and immediate context of SSR in conflict-torn societies is its contribution to peacebuilding and human security. The lack of recognition or low regard of the impact of SSR on peace processes has been one of the major causes of the resilience of armed internal conflict and 'unpeace.' Many have blamed the security sector as responsible for being the source of conflict and key obstacle to peacebuilding. First, it is an established fact that it is precisely the security forces which are at the forefront of dealing with armed insurrection and secessionist movements. They assume the 'face' of government in these conflict-ridden areas. Thus, an unprofessional security sector not subject to democratic oversight could not only increase their tendency to commit violations of human rights and international humanitarian law but could also be ineffective in the performance of their responsibilities. Misbehaving members of the armed forces could negatively affect the level of confidence or trust of the people in the government and may have dire implications for its political legitimacy.

Second, the implementation of any final settlement or resolution between the involved parties in the conflict would require the involvement and cooperation of the security sector (Greene 2003). In this regard, SSR can have a great impact on peace negotiations, as well as the final resolution and settlement of internal conflicts. A report by the UN Secretary-General notes that the 'failure to address the requirements of effective and accountable security [during peace process] can sow the seeds for future conflict' and further calls to establish a coherent approach to security reform by developing an international consensus on principles and practice for such (UNSG: 2013: 9). A study by DCAF found that between 2000 and 2015, most conflicts featured peace agreements that addressed components of SSR such as police, defense, and justice reform, albeit only a few comprehensively tackling all four SSR components, which include intelligence reform (Linke 2020).

Third, SSR not only concerns itself with the improvement of the security forces but includes the development of strong, coherent, and responsive civilian institutions. They do not merely perform democratic oversight functions but are the ones that will be responsible for most of the tasks in post-conflict peacebuilding. For example, activities related to poverty reduction, infrastructure development, and conflict resolution are often in the hands of government and possibly CSOs. This forms a significant part of addressing some of 'the roots of conflict' in which the government plays a very crucial role. SSR could also pave the way in the institutionalization of effective conflict resolution mechanisms to prevent any future conflict from erupting into violence. Thus, the strengthening of civilian agencies with functions related to SSR will be crucial in avoiding the return to conflict in the pacified areas of the country.

The current discourses on human security continue to put a premium on the role of the security sector. What has been challenged by the concept of human security is the replacement of the focus of security from the state to the individual. SSR is not at all contradictory to human security as it reorients the role of the armed forces, police, and intelligence bodies to protect the individual from threats of violence, although the concept of human security more broadly tackles chronic threats such as hunger, disease, and disruptions to daily life such as climate change (Dursun-Özkanca 2021).

Moreover, one of the most important goals of reforming security is that it may provide security for the people in an efficient and effective manner while being consistent with democracy and human rights. As already mentioned, this change was influenced by two trends felt mostly in the Global South. One is the failure of the state to guarantee the security of the people due to incompetence, inadequate resources, and poor capacity. Outbreaks of violence and order are often caused by the inability of the security sector to adequately perform their functions (Huntington 1968). Another is the fact that the security sector itself becomes the perpetrator of violence, criminality, conflict, and violations of human rights. This is common especially in countries where the armed forces and the police become instruments of the survival of authoritarian regimes (Greitens 2016). The extreme case is that the state and the security sector become indistinguishable, with force becoming the ultimate means to secure regime legitimacy and stability.

Given this, SSR focuses on contributing to the strategy of 'protection' more than 'empowerment.' It may also be dangerous that SSR completely adheres to the concept of human security, as it may have implications on the role and mandate of the security sector in the performance of functions related to the other aspects of an individual's security. An expanded definition of security containing aspects that go beyond physical security may mean that the core security forces 'dip their toes into' nontraditional areas beyond their original or intended mission and far from their training and expertise.

While SSR is inextricably linked to these tasks, it departs from the orthodox distinctions made between security, democracy, and development by integrating defense reform, police reform, intelligence reform, justice reform, legislative reform, etc. Seen as separate efforts in the past, SSR is the framework that could coordinate all these initiatives and programs into a cohesive whole. Its integrative approach and ability to group all these tasks under one roof is the source of its appeal (Forman 2006). Thus, SSR is a comprehensive process to be implemented by a multitude of institutions within the state and civil society through a series of coordinated actions and programs.

b.4. SSG/R, civil society, and local ownership

Civil society looms large in SSG. SSR ontologically looks at civil society as a positive element in ensuring accountability and responsiveness by state security forces. SSR projects are usually undertaken in post-authoritarian, weak state settings where the primary challenge of aligning security governance with broader attempts to democratize a society stems from the structural exclusion of citizens and stakeholders in formal decision-making processes. Communities are inevitable stakeholders in SSR because the endeavor revolves around reconfiguring state-society relations, as post-conflict states move away from histories that often involve systemic abuse, human rights violations, and political dominance of security forces over civilians (see Ginifer 2006 for case studies).

Corollary to this is the key objective in SSR to ensure local ownership of the reform process, consistent with the general acknowledgment that peacebuilding and reform can only be successful if it is inclusive. However, reviews of SSR in the past two decades indicate a significant gap between theory and practice. In the cases of Kosovo, Timor-Leste, Iraq, and Somalia, 'often local ownership is reduced to consultation, engagement after key decisions have been made, and involvement of only a few like-minded, state-level members of the security and political elite who accept the decisions reached previously by external actors' (Gordon 2014: 129). Mainstream evaluations of SSR see the main problem as an implementation deficit, with lack of ownership caused by the lack of bottom-up approaches, meaningful partnerships with CSOs, and sidelining of other informal security providers who are often substitutes to government service-providers in weak-state contexts (Homel & Masson 2016). This partnership is only possible if there is a values alignment between members of the security forces, political leaders, and civil society. This means that they all share the principles of good SSG. This does not mean that civil society is totally a singular actor in SSR efforts as their diversity is also important. However, groups within civil society must engage SSR with an agreement on its end goals aligned with good governance, democracy, human rights, and other principles. The next chapter discusses this important endogenous factor within civil society.

With the crisis of confidence in international development policy by the end of the 1990s due to social upheaval caused by economic structural adjustment on the one hand, and a general inability to externally catalyze state-building in the Global South on the other, the principle of 'local ownership' was endorsed in development policy more broadly and in SSR more specifically. Thus, it has already been considered that local will or commitment to SSR is deemed necessary before external intervention or assistance can be provided (Lottholz 2020). Under the Paris Declaration, local ownership by recipient states is one of the five main pillars of development aid effectiveness and is understood as beginning from the design phase of SSR interventions (Eickhoff 2021).

Donais (2018) summarizes that in SSR, the concept of local ownership is not just at the national level—between the recipient government and the donor—but also between the national government and people, a logic which is constant throughout the broader development and peacebuilding fields. This thinking has prompted the design and implementation of SSR projects to focus on inclusion, representation, and dialogues at the vertical (state-society) and horizontal (inter-society, intra-governmental) levels to maximize buy-in, and to allow societies undergoing SSR to strategize for themselves how to implement the international principles inherent in SSR in a manner consistent with local laws and public demand. In other words, if SSR is to be effective, it must be inclusive. Nathan argues that local ownership in SSR donor frameworks has evolved toward preliminary assessments on whether there is local interest in SSR and how development aid may support them, rather than thinking directly of how to execute SSR in each country (Nathan 2007).

Outside of SSR literature, however, praxis-oriented studies point to more fundamental questions about civil society and other local actors in relation to security aid policy, and consequently, more guarded perceptions of its role in political transitions. Detzner observed that there is no consensus in SSR on how to engage local actors, as many can be corrupt or use traditional practices as shields against reform (Detzner 2017). On the one hand, there is a valid point that local ownership may be reduced to token consultation or the gathering of like-minded groups and representatives if strategic frameworks and the defining principles of SSR itself are fixed by external actors and donors (Baker 2010; Krogstad 2013). To what extent can the negotiation of SSR's defining principles accommodate local views, especially those that differ from its liberal paradigm? Indeed, there has been a discussion within second-generation SSR literature about whether SSR can become truly 'post-liberal,' and whether such an approach would sacrifice the transformative vision at the expense of expediency (Sedra 2010).

In addition to this, the involvement of civil society actors presents additional complexities which, if not considered, may damage the efficacy of SSR processes and related outcomes. At a conceptual level, SSR already includes first-order norms on what it is supposed to be, namely civilian control over the military, human rights protection, and security capacity-building. Development partners from CSOs operating largely in line with international SSG principles may either not be present or may be politically marginalized in such conflict-affected contexts. Consequently, engagement of a genuinely representative cross-section of civil society opens doors for contestation of first-order principles of SSR as well as the potential for more civil conflict. In this sense, civil society is not merely an oversight actor that implements SSR. Its very involvement provides for its role as a space for new discourses that differ from or may even conflict with traditional SSR. Thus, the variation in SSR outcomes is often the function of civil society's relationship with security providers. For civil society, existing studies point to the importance of maintaining cordial relations with security actors in generating success in reform efforts (Henderson 2011).

While still supportive of general CSO involvement, Gordon (2014) nuances the argument by holding that community-based structures and mechanisms are not necessarily more legitimate, accountable, or inclusive just because they are bodies at the community level. Power asymmetries are present in many post-conflict societies, and the distribution of CSOs represents existing power relations, e.g., reflecting adversarial identity-based or political groupings, or the marginalization of groups without dense networks, thought leaders, or key champions. This is where regime type and state capacity seem to matter as intermediary factors in determining whether civil society can successfully engage SSR processes. As significant parts of the contextual environment of civil society in pursuing SSR, these two exogenous factors underscore that different types of regimes and 'stateness' of certain countries can affect whether civil society can push for SSR. For example, strong state institutions in transitioning democratic regimes can be conducive factors for civil society involvement in SSR (Scarpello 2014). Conversely, fragile states with weak or almost debilitated institutions can make civil society's work more difficult (Baker and Scheye 2007). These exogenous factors will be further discussed in the conceptual framework of this paper, as it is vital in unpacking context-specific relationships of civil society with SSR.

Some have argued that the disregard for case-to-case basis nuanced analysis of the actual state of civil society runs the risk of romanticizing civil society, without thinking of the downstream consequences of how exactly civil society shapes security governance (Uddin 2009). Caparini (in Sedra 2010) argued that even while CSOs are valued for voice, accountability, and participation, there is an unspoken assumption of the types of CSOs often engaged by state agencies and international donors, such as those that speak the development work language of logical frameworks and monitoring and evaluation. Wardak, Zama, and Nawabi (2007) point out for example that local religious and tribal leaders are not usually involved in SSR programs in the Middle East. At a conceptual level, Chanaa (2002) highlighted that there may be no single civil society to deal with, as was learned from UN engagement in the Balkans, and that much of actual reform planning deals with 'shadow networks' in civil society, such as communal associations and kinship groups. Some civil society groups have crisscrossing relations with armed actors or can themselves be eventually mobilized for violent claims-making, contentious politics, and even political change. Country case studies of SSR often point out the distrust between state security forces and civil society groups, indicating that police and military concerns against certain threat groups cannot be altogether discounted, nor is it entirely inconsistent with human rights governance (Loden 2007). This discussion emphasizes the effect of the structural composition of civil society within a given country, that while civil society is a diverse social sphere with plural social formations, specific configurations of civil society could have an influence in SSR initiatives. For example, more liberal and democratically oriented civil societies could push for SSR, compared to those whose composition is more diverse (Loada and Moderan 2015).

It is not the case that civil society should always be held suspect as a destabilizing element—as many of the problems that permeate non-state groups are also present in state forces that are unconditionally the object of security reforms. What the above discussion points out, however, is the need to better theorize about civil society in security reform contexts in a way that speaks to ground-level issues, such as fears by security agencies over a potentially destabilizing interface with civil society groups. Central to this debate is the idea of exactly how much participation can and should be allowed, and what type of actors to engage, to ensure that reforms are manageable and eventually successful. Ghimire underscores that while SSR has clear principles, it is severely lacking clear policy-relevant, context-specific pointers about *how* to implement associated programs and projects (Ghimire 2019). In this sense, SSR suffers at one level from the lack of genuine civil society involvement, and at a second level from the very thinness of conceptual thinking about civil society at the policy, programming, and implementation levels. There is a need to go beyond the rather trivial statement that 'civil society matters.'

c. Civil society and the principles and aims of SDG-16

SDG 16 aims to 'promote peaceful and inclusive societies for sustainable development, provide access to justice for all and build effective, accountable and inclusive institutions at all levels.' Much like SSG/R, scholars and practitioners have highlighted the advancement of development policy through a holistic approach, understanding that progress in other SDGs cannot be achieved without peace, inclusive justice, and strong institutions (United Nations 2013).

Rather than rally around the concept of democracy which may repel rather than secure buy-in from countries that do not meet criteria for liberal democracy, SDG-16 is framed as a bundle of good governance targets centered around critical concepts of rule of law, anti-corruption, accountability, transparency, and responsiveness. Despite the compromises in its formulation that arguably watered down its ambition, SDG-16 remains a contentious issue especially when applied to non-democratic countries and the Global South. Non-democratic regimes would find little to oppose in targets relating to reduction of violence, terrorism, and crime (Targets 16.1, 16.2, and 16.a as seen in Table 3). However, SDG-16 also involves norm cascade relating to equal access to justice (16.3), reduction of corruption and bribery (16.5), accountable and transparent institutions (16.6), inclusive and representative decision-making (16.7), and public access to information (16.10) that are deeply political processes, especially in political systems where the serious implementation of these principles goes against elite or regime interests, i.e., in contexts where bureaucracies are patrimonial, state organs are predisposed to secrecy, and where corruption is extensive. Like SSG/R, SDG-16—even if limited in its implementation—is an imposition of a standard of appropriate behavior about peace and security aspirations globally which pertain not only to efficiency, but also to procedural correctness (Ivanovic et al., 2018).

For this reason, Kempe (2019) holds that SDG-16 is one of the more innovative aspects of the SDGs because of the focus on building trust, governmental accountability, and peace sustainment—which are mostly declarations of a commitment to the *modus vivendi* rather than the ends of development per se, and these were not in the scope of the antecedent Millennium Development Goals (MDGs). It is no surprise that SDG-16's formulation was noted to be one of the more contentious aspects of the SDG process. States closely guard security and justice policy, since far-reaching reforms have extensive consequences among political elites, which makes SDG-16 prone to selective implementation, particularly its law-and-order components over its judicial and participatory targets (Nygard 2017).

Table 3: SDG-16 Targets.

16.1 Significantly reduce all forms of violence and related death rates everywhere
16.2 End abuse, exploitation, trafficking, and all forms of violence against and torture of children
16.3 Promote the rule of law at the national and international levels and ensure equal access to justice for all
16.4 By 2030, significantly reduce illicit financial and arms flows, strengthen the recovery and return of stolen assets and combat all forms of organised crime
16.5 Substantially reduce corruption and bribery in all their forms
16.6 Develop effective, accountable, and transparent institutions at all levels
16.7 Ensure responsive, inclusive, participatory, and representative decision making at all levels
16.8 Broaden and strengthen the participation of developing countries in the institutions of global governance
16.9 By 2030, provide legal identity for all, including birth registration
16.10 Ensure public access to information and protect fundamental freedoms, in accordance with national legislation and international agreements
16.a Strengthen relevant national institutions, including through international cooperation, for building capacity at all levels, in particular in developing countries, to prevent violence and combat terrorism and crime
16.b Promote and enforce non-discriminatory laws and policies for sustainable development

Source: UNGA (2015: 25–26).

The specific targets in SDG 16 are unequivocally facilitative of the creation, development, and protection of civil society, specifically in access to justice and information, the demand for accountable institutions, and goals which embed in them fundamental freedoms against violence and torture. At the most fundamental level, SDGs in general begin with a people-centered, results-oriented outlook, which is why civil society looms large in its implementation process. SDG-16 therefore adopts a conventional view of civil society as a form of communicative arena within which preferences can be marshaled, with its role of providing alternative views for the consideration of state actors. Dattler (2016: 20) writes on various roles that can be performed by civil society in the SDGs:

> Civil society stakeholders can take on a variety of functions in the implementation process. They can spur government action through persistent advocacy and act as watchdogs holding governments accountable to their commitments. They can advise governments on concrete implementation measures to take, building on their experience on the ground, often working with marginalized communities. Civil society organizations can also directly support implementation through the role they often play in service delivery, including in the area of sexual and reproductive health, and can have an important role in supporting data collection efforts, including on marginalized groups.

Some have noted the inherent limitation to this approach, which treats SDG-16 implementation as ultimately a state-based endeavor where civil society is enlisted insofar as it will help advance the agenda. For example, the Transparency, Accountability, and Participation Network —a global network of non-governmental organizations working on SDG-16 and the 2030 Agenda—has noted two vital points: the first is that governments tend to be the sole evaluators of their own performance since they ultimately control the access by CSOs to the review process, and second is that actual CSO participation in the implementation—the level of commitment needed, defined, and allowed with respect to national jurisdictions—is not properly defined. SOLIDAR (2021) added in its review of CSO and human rights protection under SDG-16 and 17 that there are few legal obligations on the part of the government to involve CSOs in policymaking; the extent of inclusion depends on the style of the executive or comfortability of the political system.

Three insights emerge from a review of observations about civil society participation in SDG-16 implementation. First, SDG-16 dealing with peace, justice, and 'strong institutions' is not necessarily a coherent vision, with the actions toward peace and security sometimes proving detrimental to inclusion and broad-based civil society participation. For example, SDG 16a specifically tackles the prevention of violence and combatting of terrorism and crime, which have existing arrangements that have been observed to conflict directly with civil society empowerment—another equally important component of SDG-16. For instance, numerous evaluations of Anti-Money Laundering/Countering Terrorist Financing (AML-CTF) frameworks have emphasized the downstream harms for civic space due to the added administrative burdens for extensive background checks and undemocratic state proscriptions of terrorist designations. While AML-CTF regulations are understandable, such regulations can also become barriers to entry for CSOs in places where building such networks is nascent and highly vulnerable (Ibezim-Ohaeri, n.d.). To be fair, there have been critical reforms by the Financial Action Task Force (FATF) to ensure an adequate balance between de-risking from potential conduits of terrorist financing and ensuring that such regulations are not weaponized by governments to curtail civil society—as is often the case in non-democratic countries that use CSO registration guidelines against foreign interference as a pretext to deter independent CSO activity (NYU Paris Public Interest Clinic 2021). There is a valid concern that SDG-16 as adopted at the national level is prone to securitization, especially with programs related to preventing and countering violent extremism (CT/PCVE) in the aftermath of the Global War on Terror. A parallel development worth highlighting is the so-called 're-securitization' of security assistance especially by the United States that poured funding into military arms transfers and capacity-building without a symmetrical focus on human rights obligations due to the need to work with non-democratic states in accosting terrorists. SDG-16 targets have been criticized for being poorly formulated, with the rule of law components eclipsing transparency and public participation in the implementation of SDG-16, which makes the agenda prone to securitization (Lazarus 2020; Ramcharan 2021).

Second, there is still relatively unsophisticated thinking about how to engage civil society in SDG-16 because of the lack of proper conceptualization, leading to poorly fleshed-out implementation strategies. For one thing, CIVICUS (2017a.) found that despite the extensive grassroots mobilizational capacity of political parties, there is little evidence of meaningful engagement with them under the SDGs. In many fragile and conflict-affected contexts, civil society, conventionally understood by Alagappa (2004) as a distinct space for organization by non-state, non-market groups that take civil collective action to influence the state, does not exist. Many community-based organizations that are the most politically influential may be excluded from engagement since they are not 'civil society' conventionally understood—and sometimes rightfully so—due to lack of genuine autonomy from political elites and state sponsorship. Sénit (2020) posited that larger, more established CSOs do not view formal processes in the SDG consultations as venues for influence, but rather as epiphenomenal to the influence they already have in prior engagements with government, since most meetings of SDGs took place beyond negotiating sessions.

Consequently, a third critical point is that the inclusiveness of 'civil society' itself needs to be thoroughly reviewed to ensure that consultations are value-adding and not tokenistic. Several components of SDG-16 on crime control (16a) and reduction of private violence (16.1 and 16.2) run the risk of easily being securitized by states for strategic-military purposes. While tasks in peacebuilding are still properly in the realm of development work, the background of development professionals working on technical issues such as penal reform or transnational crime are often drawn from military, police, criminal justice, intelligence, and government-insiders. Without careful attention to the balance in perspectives and the professional mix, SDG-16 runs the risk of being dominated by traditional security thinking (Dursun-Özkanca 2021).

Another angle to this is at the level of civil society organizations enveloped by the SDG-16 drive to include CSOs in the well-intentioned goal of inclusive security decision-making. In a review of counterterrorism policy in the Philippines, Arugay et al. (2021) observed that there seemed to be initial signs of harmful 'instrumentalization' of civil society not as co-providers but as another tool for program implementation. At the level of governments, National Action Plans tend to utilize state-centric approaches and exclusivist visions for how civil society could be integrated in the CT/PCVE paradigm. Especially in conflicts with substantial international participation, this reinforces the perception that foreign governments are using local peace activists to the detriment of the conflict-vulnerable society. At the level of society, CSOs working on peace and development have also been pressured to align programs with CT/PCVE goals and targets, which has narrowed down the focus of interventions to preventing recruitment and radicalization, rather than the broader gamut of structural issues (e.g., corruption, abuse by state forces) that drive violent extremism (Saferworld 2019).

To be sure, this problem lies not solely with SDG-16 but with the broader international environment for security assistance and development aid. The messy relationship of civil society, private actors, and state forces is part of country-specific development work. In some cases, the insistence of engagement toward certain types of think tank-like CSOs or rights-protection advocacy groups runs the risk of engaging actors that are not genuinely representative of grassroots constituencies (Sénit 2020). In its review of human rights protection in El Salvador, SOLIDAR (2021) found that the value of CSOs and human rights defenders needed to be explained first to the wider public for these ideas to gain local traction, indicating the public belief that these values are not necessarily universally salient or widely held (SOLIDAR 2021).

Implicit in such treatment of CSOs is the understanding that they are oversight actors, often to the neglect of the fact that they become power brokers in their own right. A critical case is the observation by many international non-governmental organizations that civil society becomes a direct security provider in weak state contexts. For example, in several conflict-affected areas, clans—being cultural units—maintain private security networks that mediate social, economic, and legal disputes among the population (Saferworld 2016). In contexts where neither government nor the armed opposition effectively rule, civil society becomes the main conduit for alternative governance. In Afghanistan, civil society engaged in civilian protection by directly transacting with armed groups. The normalization of relations required establishing credibility, mainly with civil society distancing itself from the state and also taking it upon itself to provide for the defense of their communities.

d. SSG/R, SDG-16, and civil society

Both SSG/R and SDG-16 are results of the gradual reorientation of peace and security concepts in the last three decades toward 'human security,' as opposed to conventional regime or state security, and the understanding that the management of peace, justice, and security will require a value-laden transformative agenda rooted in liberal norm-institutionalization, rather than apolitical, capability-oriented technical assistance. Both concepts are linked by the centrality of human security in development planning which looks at human needs in economic, health, environmental, personal, community, and political spheres to privilege threats to average citizens, rather than just to the state (Dursun-Özkanca 2021). Consequently, it expands the focus of security assistance in development and aid policy thinking by drawing attention to non-traditional concerns relating to structural factors, rather than merely direct violence which threatens the survival, livelihood, and dignity of people.

Conceptually, human security embeds the field of security with critical norms about economic, civil, political, and social rights which form the corpus of norms that guide SSG/R and SDG-16, such as inclusiveness, accountability, rule of law, responsiveness, and legitimacy. Some have argued that the expansion of focus in the security-development field toward justice and the subsequent 'developmentalization' of security away from traditional state-centric concerns has spurred an ambitious and transformative agenda of democratic state-building (Sedra 2010). As noted in the earlier subsection in SSG/R, material capability-building such as the purchase of equipment and financial support for personnel professionalization is the mainstream understanding of security assistance, prior to the infusion of key development concepts such as transitional justice and grievance mechanisms. Both SDG-16 and SSR—in touching the issue of good governance—follow the liberal peacebuilding approach which seeks partially or wholly to go beyond a 'train and equip' status quo by setting sights on the importance of altering power relations, opening policy circles, and formalizing civilian protection concepts in broader security doctrine (Donais 2018). Both SDG-16 and SSR comprise what could be referred to as a norm mainstreaming approach to peacebuilding, with civil society empowerment and inclusion being a common condition. Many studies have covered the extensive efforts of development workers and peace advocates toward increasing the voice of non-state actors in government consultations.

In this sense, SDG-16 and SSR concepts provide the conceptual basis for the inclusion of civil society as an integral component of any peace, justice, and security reform process. In the main, civil society takes on three principal roles in conceptualizing and implementing SDG-16 and SSR projects: (1) an agent of democratic accountability and civilian oversight; (2) a space for new discourses on security and development; and (3) an alternative provider of people-oriented security (see Section 3B of this paper for a full discussion). Countries and communities substantially differ in their implementation of SDG-16 and SSR principles, which sometimes leads to asymmetries or different foci that affect the overall nature of the reform process.

SSR in general prescribes not only outcomes, but specific organizational forms and key reforms that must be undertaken. As outlined in this paper (see Table 1), at the conceptual level, SSR offers a clear set of areas of concern (civilian control, capacity-building, cooperation) that can each tackle specific ways and means in terms of political, economic, social, and institutional reforms. Strong criticisms levied against SSR involve not the goals or 'bucket list' of reforms, but rather the deficits in operational-level implementation. In contrast, while SDG-16 is an analogous set of goals, there is a lack of clear references to political processes and democratic reforms in how targets might be achieved, thereby limiting the set of specific commitments that civil society actors could claim from the state (Zamfir 2020). El Baradei (2020) points out that only 6 of the 23 indicators of SDG-16 targets are considered as Tier I, or those that are conceptually clear, have an established agreed methodology, and were created by many countries around the world. To be sure, some components of SDG-16 on access to information (16.10) and the participation of stakeholders from the Global South in relevant institutions for global governance (16.8) relate clearly to concrete reform programs.

At another level, there is an argument that because security and peace programs have well-defined goals, there is a minimal amount of actual local co-determination in the conceptualization and implementation, especially in strong state, weak society contexts and conflict-affected areas (Bendix and Stanley 2008). Second, both SSR and SDG-16 see civil society as partners in the implementation of its agenda, though there appears to be a lack of dedicated analysis to the concept and how it fits both agenda.

There are some key takeaways from academic and policy studies. First, there is a need to reconcile oftentimes conflicting voices within civil society, who have different security needs and interests. There is a perception among security practitioners that expanding the number of actors involved satisfies inclusivity but also potentially makes programs vulnerable to spoilers (Cubitt 2013). Additionally, as in the case of Indonesia, security forces may themselves enjoy high public trust, which makes efforts for greater transparency and sectoral reform more costly since upsetting power distributions is seen as unwelcoming interference (Heiduk 2014). Recent reviews of the state of civil society around the world note the shrinking democratic space for reasons that go beyond SSR and SDG-16, including the decreasing public belief in democracy, populist attacks against liberal-democratic principles, and sheer opportunism by authoritarian political figures (CIVICUS 2019. Relatedly, the ideological roots and donor concentration for SSR and SDG-16 programs in Western countries are often portrayed by autocrats as a form of foreign influence. Scholars have noted that funding for SSR and SDG-16 projects often comes from developed Western countries who often look quickly for like-minded local partners, and understandably so given the desirability of the rule of law, an accountable security sector, and effective public participation in policy formulation (Sedra 2010). These observations point to the existing dynamic where there is an appearance of foreign sponsorship of specific actors within civil society without the effort to gain broad-based acceptance first.

Another related issue is that CSOs are self-appointed rather than elected. If they are tapped into SSR and SDG-16 projects, this often creates a local perception of an accountability or legitimacy deficit. Compounding this is donor dynamics, since funding and resources are mostly provided to these organizations, where they can be seen as more accountable to advance foreign rather than local agendas, as has been the argument in India, Egypt, Macedonia, and Turkey, among others (Hayes 2017). Authoritarian regimes have been keen to restrict the registration of CSOs under the guise of counter-terrorist financing frameworks and to condition public opinion not only against foreign donors, but against local CSOs that champion democracy and human rights—agendas that often stand in opposition to political leaders.

Second, some have pointed out the danger of integrating the concept of 'informal security and justice mechanisms' into SSR and SDG-16, so as not to romanticize engagement with non-state actors, organizations, and even community justice mechanisms—which themselves are not necessarily more inclusive or compliant with human rights principles on the mere basis that they are local organization practices—whilst still calling for the concept of informal security and justice mechanisms to be integrated in mainstream SSR and SDG-16 (Ansorg and Gordon 2019). To compound this, there exists no consensus on how to incorporate local actors who use practices that contravene key SSR and SDG principles—or are themselves corrupt—into broader justice and reform processes. The relationship between non-state and civil society actors with peace and justice initiatives has been argued to be tricky in the absence of a consensus on how to incorporate them in contexts where local actors use traditional practices that contravene key SSR and SDG principles or can themselves be corrupt (Detzner 2017). Rather than a pretext to justify the exclusion of civil society, the more nuanced approach within development and peacebuilding was to identify how and when to engage civil society and groups therein. As Gordon (2014) argues, 'locals' do not constitute a homogeneous whole with shared security interests and concerns; conflict-affected areas are precisely marked by deep-seated differences. Critically, these debates about the terms of enlistment of civil society in peacebuilding are absent from mainstream SSG/R/SSR and SDG-16 literature, as well as major policy and donor documents.

Third, in practice civil society sometimes becomes a neutral or third party in conflict zones because it is their independence from the state which affords them some degree of leniency by warring parties, insurgents, or terrorists to negotiate projects such as Civilian Protection Councils that serve as a voice for the community in dealing with armed actors—a function that requires neutrality so as not to instigate reprisal by parties to the conflict or combatant groups (CIVIC 2019). However, this requires civil society to be able to transact with insurgents, risking that they be perceived as insurgent collaborators by the state, as was the case in Afghanistan and Iraq (CIVIC 2019). At the same time, the previously mentioned risk of being instrumentalized by the state as implementers of essentially pro-state security programs such as PCVE could undermine civil society's credibility among local actors and lead to informant dynamics.

CHAPTER III

Analytical Framework: Civil Society as an Oversight Agent, Space for Discourse, and Alternative Security Provider

This chapter discusses the paper's analytical framework that will be utilized to analyze the various empirical case studies. This framework is composed of three interconnected parts: (1) the endogenous and exogenous factors to civil society that affect its ability to influence SSG/R processes; (2) the three primary roles played by civil society in promoting SSG/R; and (3) the three main consequences of civil society's SSG/R roles to the realization of SDG-16.

a. Civil society's endogenous and exogenous factors

This paper adopts a broader view of civil society as it is open-ended to the actual goals and behavioral dispositions of civil society, but at the same time distinguishes it from the state and political society (political parties, insurgents, and elites) whose aim is to capture state power. Empirically, these types of CSOs are usually social movements, trade unions, advocacy NGOs, peasant federations, and associations of students, intellectuals, and laborers etc. They represent sectors within society, engage in political activities, and resort to collective action such as protests to express collective demands. In practice, however, these organizations form coalitions with or engage state and armed actors (White 2004).

As mentioned in this paper's introductory chapter, the extant scholarly literature often attributed civil society's power to influence governance processes as resting on the interplay of factors within civil society as well as those found outside its sphere. These endogenous or internal factors refer to the *structural composition and values* shared by members of civil society. Civil

How to cite this book chapter:
Arugay, A. A. & Baquisal, J. K. A. 2024. *Accountability, Discourse, and Service Provision: Civil Society's Roles in Security Sector Governance and Reform (SSG/R) and Sustainable Development Goal-16 (SDG-16).* Pp. 29–33. London: Ubiquity Press. DOI: https://doi.org/10.5334/bcy.c. License: CC-BY-NC

society's structural composition refers to the size, plurality, and robustness of its member organizations. It could be argued that a large civil society composed of diverse organizations which are autonomous from the state could potentially make positive contributions to SSG/R. However, one cannot make a linear and direct causal connection between civil society's sheer size with its ability to influence policy reform processes, as there are other factors that should be considered in determining causality.

The second endogenous factor refers to the values represented and advocated by CSOs engaged in SSG/R advocacy. This refers to civil society's normative and cultural orientation, particularly whether it seeks to pursue the principles of SSG/R as discussed in Chapter 2. The more that civil society actors imbibe and put into practice these principles such as accountability, responsiveness, inclusivity, and transparency, the more they are in a better position to advocate SSG/R (Caparini and Fluri 2006).

To be effective advocates, the internal factors within civil society must work together with its political environment which must likewise be conducive to SSG/R. There are three exogenous factors relevant for civil society: (1) *regime type*; (2) level of *state capacity*; and (3) civil society's *relations with security providers*. The regime type refers to the nature of the political regime of a given country, whether it is more or less democratic. State capacity concerns the ability of the political institutions, particularly the government, to impose legitimate order and control in society. Countries with lingering internal conflict or insurgencies therefore reflect lower levels of state capacity. Finally, relations with security providers such as the military are an important contextual factor since it pertains to whether CSOs have a working partnership with these security sector institutions to be able to work on SSR. The overall expectation for a conducive exogenous environment for potentially successful SSG/R outcomes depends on whether the civil society lies within a more democratic regime that has a higher level of state capacity and has good working relationships with security providers (Forman 2006; Caparini in Sedra 2010).

b. Three primary roles of CSOs in SSG/R

Civil society's endogenous and exogenous factors serve as the background and environment that determine the specific role/s they will play in promoting SSG/R processes. As mentioned in Chapter 1, these three main roles are: (1) *an agent of democratic accountability and civilian oversight*; (2) *a space for new discourses on security and development*; and (3) *an alternative provider of people-oriented security*. This paper does not specifically advocate for an exclusive emphasis on any of the three roles above; rather, its goal is to empirically unpack these different conceptions of civil society that are reflected in how SDG-16 and SSR programs are designed. Each role has its own merits and risks. Additionally, relational aspects in the configuration of these different concepts—such as the emphasis of one over the other—also create their own *sui generis* challenges. For example, as noted in the literature review, an emphasis on civil society being managers of development projects or support groups for the government's plans without a concomitant voice in the formulation of policy action plans can lead to the instrumentalization of civil society in an otherwise state-centric agenda that fosters human insecurity.

The first role of civil society as an oversight actor draws heavily from the liberal tradition of acting as a bulwark against the overwhelming power of the state as discussed in Chapter 2. In this conceptualization, civil society is often seen as a monolithic actor with shared values and norms acting as a check on the government's exercise of its mandate. This can also be viewed as the mainstream view in looking at civil society in security and development. Its autonomy from the state, outsider status, and ability to collectively organize make it the default ballast against political authority (Edwards and Foley 1998).

Among the three roles, civil society's oversight function has received the most attention from scholars and practitioners of SSG/R. Under this role, CSOs serve as a mobilizer of popular support and opposition to serve as a guardrail against non-responsive and non-inclusive policymaking. They are in a unique position to implement projects that require community trust, voice the concerns of local communities and drive effective campaigns toward the state and society (Rauch 2011). The necessity for this is highlighted by the lack of transparency in government behavior in conflict zones (Malik 2009).

Though many in the security sector and the donor community view most civil societies as an informal source of civilian oversight, CSOs have not limited themselves to this role. Over time, civil society began to also perform the role of a space for alternative security discourses. This stemmed from the increasing diversity of CSOs participating in SSG/R, as well as the realities that they faced in societies that do not normally conform to the conventional expectations on state capacity, regime stability, and hybridity of security conditions (Schroeder et al. 2014).

This role advances the idea that CSOs could be a catalyst for alternative thinking on achieving SSG/R. For example, framings about how peacebuilding ought to be conducted could be formed from a genuinely human security perspective rather than traditional elite-focused security (Ibezim-Ohaeri, n.d.). This is deeply related to knowledge production, although separates from it since the function relates more to an autonomous sphere of agenda-setting from the state, rather than the precursor knowledge-production per se. Saferworld observes that one problem in recent years at least for P/CVE projects has been the trend to see civil society and locals as objects for reform and targets of programs, diminishing their meaningful input to the process (Saferworld 2019).

Civil society's discursive role can be seen in two ways: (a) generation of *research and publications* that shape alternative security discourse and substantive content of SSR, and (b) the *training* of independent experts and practitioners who have backgrounds in novel, non-traditional, and participatory security approaches. For example, SSG/R projects often involve monitoring and evaluation components. At the programmatic level, the demand for the collection of data necessitates that civil society acquire the skills and resources for research and information dissemination, which are institutional precursors to holding the government accountable.

The third role is relatively the most novel of the ways in which civil society pursues SSG/R. Civil society becomes an *alternative provider of people-oriented security* itself. Rather than work with the security forces and other actors within the security sector, CSOs are providing this public good themselves. The key contexts for this role to emerge can range from fragile and conflict-affected states and the destruction of the entire security sector to the existence of gaps in the provision of security. CIVICUS reports that citizen-generated data for SDG-16 indicate that most CSOs were engaged in standing up against civilian harm, as well as in community-based development projects that address symptoms and causes of conflict (CIVICUS 2019). Local actors often fill in security vacuums in weak state contexts and become security co-providers with the state through local mediation mechanisms, community security groups, and early response arrangements. The extent to which this reality clashes with often Weberian notions of the state as the primary security provider in SSR and SDG literature, and the theoretical relegation of civil society for input or interest articulation functions, has been noted in the previous two subsections. Some have argued that the use of civil society as a participant in unconventional security arrangements is valuable not just because it enhances participation, but also that it reduces the load on formal institutions to handle variegated social demands and enable the provision of public goods without necessarily relying on state initiative (Ghimire 2019). However, this emergent role calls into question the civil and nonviolent nature of CSOs. If social organizations possess the means of violence, then how can they remain within the sphere of civil society? Given that this nascent role has been observed by this paper, it needs more information on how this role is actually realized. As a 'first stab' at

Table 4: Civil Society Roles in SSG/R.

Analytical Framework	DCAF Version	Main Activities
Agent of democratic accountability and oversight	Monitoring and public oversight	– Oversee performance of the security sector – Raise alarms over possible abuse or wrongdoing ('watchdog' function) – Collaborate with media and other non-state actors with oversight functions
Space for security discourse	Awareness raising	– Conduct information dissemination/campaigns about the security sector – Promote new ideas about security provision – Update security sector on the latest developments in SSG/R
	Advocacy	– Train security sector in SSG/R concepts and principles – Represent marginalized voices in security dialogues and conversations – Promote more inclusive SSG/R activities
	Fact-finding, research, and analysis	– Conduct research and publications – Collaborate with media to investigate and study SSG/R processes – Monitor and evaluate state of SSG
Provider of people-oriented security	Service provision	– Provide services that support security provision – Conduct training to improve security provision in accordance with SSG/R principles – Help safeguard communities in precarious security situations

analyzing this role, this paper is limited in evaluating whether this role could be legitimately accepted, as more research is required.

These three roles also fit quite well with DCAF's own conceptualization of the main civil society activities that seek to improve SSG/R (see Table 4). The table below integrates the paper's own formulation of CSO roles with DCAF's conceptualization.[1]

c. Impact of civil society's SSG/R roles on SDG-16

The last component of this paper's analytical framework concerns the linkages between civil society's roles in promoting SSG/R as a contribution to meeting some of the targets set by SDG-16. As there are ten specific targets, this paper argues that civil society's SSG/R efforts have the most impact in improving the implementation of the principles of accountability, transparency, and participation (See Table 5). In fact, these three principles have direct connections with specific SDG-16 targets:

1. *Accountability*: Develop effective, accountable, and transparent institutions at all levels (16.6)

---

[1] The author thanks the reviewers from DCAF for this suggestion.

Table 5: Civil Society Roles in SSG/R and SDG-16 Targets.

Role of Civil Society	SDG-16 Target		
	Accountability (16.6)	*Transparency (16.10)*	*Participation (16.7)*
Agent of democratic oversight and accountability	Primary	Primary	Secondary
Space for security discourse	Secondary	Secondary	Primary
Provider of people-oriented security	Secondary	Primary	Primary

2. *Transparency*: Ensure public access to information and protect fundamental freedoms, in accordance with national legislation and international agreements (16.10); and
3. *Participation*: Ensure responsive, inclusive, participatory, and representative decision-making at all levels (16.7).

The juxtaposition of the role of civil society in SSG/R and SDG-16 targets is analyzed using an approach that emphasizes whether each role has a primary or secondary contribution to a specific principle behind an SDG-16 target. If a CSO becomes an agent of democratic oversight and accountability, it has a primary contribution to accountability and transparency. This is done because of the sheer size of the security sector, as well as the mandate of security institutions to provide peace and security. Secondarily, it can also fulfill the target of participation if this role is performed with democratic consultation and involvement of other social and political actors. By implementing people-centric participation, civil society efforts to promote SSG/R could strengthen political institutions which is critical to realizing SDG-16.

On the other hand, if civil society becomes a space for security discourse, it has a greater impact in meeting the participation target (16.7). This is due to the ability of civil society to invite other stakeholders and convene them in a space where discussions could take place on issues, problems, and solutions to insecurity. This role could also help provide alternative or human security frameworks and achieve sustainable peace and security. By acting as a forum for deliberation, civil society could encourage innovative solutions to problems of insecurity that depart from state-centric or traditional militarized approaches.

Finally, if it acts as a provider of people-oriented security, it could primarily contribute toward transparency since this initiative is a marked departure from conventional and state-centric approaches to security provision. Such conventional approaches could then be centralized and not customized to the needs and problems of communities. Civil society actors and their partners are in a better position to provide security not only anchored to the actual needs of citizens but ensuring that this is in keeping with human rights standards.

It could be argued that civil society also has a prominent role to play in meeting other SDG-16 targets, but for the purposes of this paper it chose to focus on these three main targets, given their good fit with SSG/R principles. This notion is also supported by a seminal study that made explicit linkage between SSG/R and SDG-16 such as:

> through promoting greater institutionalization and good governance principles, as well as its focus on reforming the security and justice institutions, by forming a closer connection between states and their populations. It may also help with its emphasis on good governance and capacity development (Dursun-Özkanca 2021: 55).

This paper's analytical framework will be used in presenting the case studies in the next chapter.

CHAPTER IV

Case Studies

This chapter focuses on actual case studies of CSOs engaged in promoting SSG/R. This case study approach was chosen to highlight the dynamics behind the various roles played by civil society as an agent of civilian oversight, space for security discourse, and an alternative provider of security. As mentioned in the introductory chapter, the rationale behind purposive selection of the Philippines, Tunisia, and several fragile and conflict-affected states is to emphasize the endogenous and exogenous factors that contribute to which roles civil society played in SSG/R activities. It must be noted that these countries are not all fully fledged cases of successful or purely positive SSG/R outcomes. For the most part, the cases are complex experiences of mixed results. SSG/R gains from civil society engagements often present new challenges, while structural impediments and obstacles are identified that hinder the ability of civil society to effectively advocate reforms for good security sector governance and in turn, help achieve SDG-16. Finally, this paper utilizes the case studies to shed light on how CSOs could fulfill a specific role. In particular, the Philippines highlights the ability of civil society to be an agent of democratic accountability and oversight, while Tunisia shows how CSOs could use their sphere as a space for security discourses. Finally, the cases of some fragile and conflict-affected states call into attention the ways in which some societal actors are providing people-oriented security as a service to their communities, and the challenges such situations present for SSG at large.

The case of the Philippines (2010–2020) represents a mixed outcome of success then rollback of SSR. Prior to 2015, there were some major strides in implementing reforms for good SSG with the help of civil society as an agent of democratic accountability and oversight. However, the flaws in the country's democracy led to a regression in terms of good SSG. The momentum for further reforms did not last as the deficits in civil society participation accentuated the security challenges in the Philippines from 2016 onwards, a post-transition country still beset with international security threats emanating from a communist insurgency and secessionist movements (Arugay

---

How to cite this book chapter:
Arugay, A. A. & Baquisal, J. K. A. 2024. *Accountability, Discourse, and Service Provision: Civil Society's Roles in Security Sector Governance and Reform (SSG/R) and Sustainable Development Goal-16 (SDG-16).* Pp. 35–53. London: Ubiquity Press. DOI: https://doi.org/10.5334/bcy.d. License: CC-BY-NC

et al. 2021). Under the administration of populist leader Rodrigo Duterte, the country underwent democratic erosion and the heightened presence of the military as a security provider in aspects of civilian governance (Arugay 2021). This had a significant impact in how the Philippines trailed in meeting the targets set by SDG-16 (Reyes et al. 2019).

In Tunisia, there was a mixed record of success and failure as the country rebuilt its security sector after the 2011 revolution that toppled dictatorial rule. As a transitioning country, Tunisia showed the many challenges of democratizing the relations between civilian politicians and the security sector. This was where its emergent civil society became active. Through its efforts, civil society pushed for a more democratic constitution that enshrined SSR principles as well as civil society participation in governance. In other words, where no space existed before, civil society became a catalyst for the creation of the conditions necessary for their involvement in security governance. However, the challenges of violent extremism, limited pluralism, economic stagnation, and intra-civil society tensions all indicated that the pursuit of SSG/R in Tunisia was still a work in progress.

Finally, the third case focuses on conflict-torn states such as Somalia where there was the relatively novel phenomenon of groups affiliated with civil society undertaking service provision, particularly people-oriented security. This might confound the conventional expectations about the appropriate roles that civil society performs in SSG. In Somalia, as the state ceased to function in providing security, it became incumbent for CSOs to help their communities by attending to their security needs or acting as brokers between them and non-state armed groups. This set-up could be viewed as nowhere near the ideal situation where the state provides for the security needs of its people with civil society acting as a source of support and provider of civilian oversight; this was because the failure of governance and huge gaps in security provision in these conflict-ridden states pushed CSOs to perform unorthodox roles to serve and protect their constituents. This set of cases also examines the risks of heavily relying on CSOs as security providers and the far-reaching implications on SSG and realizing SDG-16.

a. Civil society in the Philippines: providing oversight and accountability

The case of the Philippines showed that its civil society could have a positive role in SSR through its ability to provide informal oversight and accountability. This was due to its robust set of CSOs that were bounded by democratic principles, cordial relations with the security forces, and its democratic government. The pursuit of SSR had an impact in meeting several of the targets of SDG-16. However, the Philippines also revealed that such gains could be undermined by populist governments bent on militarizing governance by mobilizing security forces to perform nontraditional political roles without civilian oversight and accountability.

a.1. Endogenous factors

The Philippines has one of the most vibrant, robust, dynamic, and politically active civil societies in the world. Several cases proved its efficacy in providing policy inputs, delivering social services, pursuing socioeconomic development, and generating accountability. CSOs exercised considerable power vis-à-vis the Philippine state in pressing demands for popular causes such as good governance, social justice, and sustainable development. With its deep affinity with democracy, Filipino civil society became a reliable bulwark against abuses of state power and endemic corruption in government (Cariño 2002; Clarke 2000. As Asia's oldest democracy, the Philippines maintained a dense civil society engaged at the top echelons of governance, while still very much grounded from below as its many organizations retained their grassroots character.

Philippine civil society was a product of the country's struggle against Marcos' constitutional authoritarian regime from 1972 to 1986. Civil society was significantly shaped by the 'dangerous, heady experience of organizing oppressed people under martial law' (Racelis 2000). Despite these repressive conditions, CSOs steadily flourished, extending their networks and incrementally building an infrastructure of political contention against the government. A glaring display of civil society's power was demonstrated in a grand display of nonviolent collective action, known as the 1986 People Power revolt, which ended Marcos' dictatorial regime (Thompson 1995). The 1987 Constitution and subsequent legal instruments provided civil society with access to important policy processes. Therefore, in terms of civil society's endogenous factors, the Philippine case is an example of a robust, dynamic, and plural civil society.

a.2. Exogenous factors

Coexisting with a vibrant civil society is a problematic domestic security environment. The Philippines is no stranger to internal conflict. For centuries, the country experienced significant security issues within its domestic borders, from insurgencies and terror attacks to outright military occupation. The twin internal challenges of a nationwide resilient communist insurgency and a Muslim separatist movement in the southern island of Mindanao led to instability throughout the archipelago. The conflicts had deep-seated causes going back to the colonial era which continued under post-independence governments and perpetuated unequal access to social services and economic development, as well as aggressive counterinsurgency policies. Such state abuses, combined with poor and unequal social service delivery, glaring economic inequality, and widespread political exclusion, fed the grievances of minority religious and ethnic groups, as well as people living in rural poverty. To date, these internal conflicts constitute the most serious domestic security challenge in the Philippines (Arugay et. al. 2021).

Prior to 2010, the relationship between civil society and security providers such as the military was fraught with challenges. Much of this had something to do with the country's experience of martial law. The country's armed forces became the partner of the Marcos dictatorship in the implementation of autocratic rule. This resulted in rampant violations of the human rights of activists and members of civil society (Arugay 2008).

On the other hand, the country's security providers were suspicious of the motives and actions of civil society. They were seen as front organizations of leftist groups that had alleged links with the armed communist movement. The Armed Forces of the Philippines (AFP) would often scorn CSOs because of their socialist tendencies and strategies of contentious politics, often construed as sources of security threats. This perception of the security forces significantly eroded civil society-military relations (Tyner 2005; Hedman 2006; Arugay 2021).

A reform-oriented government led by President Benigno Simeon Aquino from 2010 to 2016 provided an opportunity for improved relations between civil society and the military. His presidency focused on curbing corruption and implementing governance reforms, with the help of leaders from civil society assuming important cabinet portfolios in social development, peace processes, and even security policy. Transparency and accountability became the operating principles of the administration, and this was diffused throughout the country's security sector (Chambers 2014).

Since 2010, the Philippine government embarked on SSR initiatives to improve the military's effectiveness and accountability. SSR is a major principle stated in the country's National Security Policy since the Benigno Aquino III Administration (2010–2016). This push for professionalism and democratic accountability by the country's civilian leadership coupled with the military's voluntary cooperation increased public trust and confidence in the military. A December 2019 poll revealed that the AFP enjoyed its highest trust ratings since public opinion polling began. An astounding 79% of Filipinos trusted the military (Arugay 2021).

The steady improvement of the military's image among Filipinos was a by-product of its openness to embrace reform and substantive professionalism. Among others, this included setting up human rights offices across the military establishment; the adoption of a transformation roadmap with the guidance of reputable members of the civilian bureaucracy, academe, media, and civil society; and cooperating with politicians to deal with peace and development challenges at the local level. When the military formulated its anti-insurgency program named the Internal Peace and Security Plan-*Bayanihan*[1] (IPSP-*Bayanihan*), it included strong participation from civil society groups. CSOs worked with security providers in implementing these changes. For example, leaders of NGOs, academics, and other reputable members of civil society became part of the AFP's Multi-Sectoral Advisory Board which has counterparts in all the major services of the Philippine military. The critical inputs of civil society were stressed by President Aquino's peace process adviser, Teresita Quintos-Deles, who herself was a longtime civil society leader and SSR advocate when she said:

> As far as the security sector reforms instituted by the AFP are concerned, partnerships and multi-stakeholder cooperation on a shared vision are at work. This is a huge transformation and a milestone for Philippine democracy…Especially since our focus is on developing democratic control of armed forces, the call is to make ordinary citizens understand that what happens in the security sector will have an effect on their lives (Official Gazette of the Republic of the Philippines 2012: 1).

a.3. CSO roles

An example of an SSG/R initiative where civil society played the role as an agent of democratic accountability and oversight was *Bantay Bayanihan* (BB) [*Bayanihan* Watch]. Launched in 2011, the BB established a permanent forum for civil society-military-police coordination and civil society oversight of the security sector. BB engaged the security sector in critical and constructive collaboration by serving as an independent oversight body in the implementation of the AFP IPSP-*Bayanihan*. Like SSR principles, it adopted a 'Whole of Nation Approach' involving many diverse stakeholders as well as local ownership. Its 15 clusters nationwide included 150 CSOs—including human rights, religious, environmental, academic, and labor groups—together with civilian government units and leaders from the main executive agencies of the government. An independent think tank, the Security Reform Initiative (SRI), served as the BB's national secretariat (Schirch and Macini-Griffoli 2015).

BB aimed for dialogue partners to jointly implement the IPSP-*Bayanihan* to ensure and advance human rights, international humanitarian law, rule of law, accountability, civilian

---

[1] *Bayanihan* is a Filipino term that roughly translates to a spirit of civic unity and cooperation. It is a core part of the Filipino cultural value-system.

engagement, and democratization of the armed forces. Specifically, BB included the following tasks:

1. Serving as a venue or direct channel to raise issues regarding the IPSP-*Bayanihan*, including peace and security concerns of local communities.
2. Conducting and validating periodic evaluations of IPSP-*Bayanihan*.
3. Providing recommendations to the Chief of Staff (national level) and Commanding General (unified command/division/brigade level) on IPSP-*Bayanihan*.
4. Generating concise policy recommendations on security reforms together with peace and conflict dynamics, to be submitted and presented to respective peace and order councils (local executive) and *sanggunian* (local legislative), all the way to national-level Cabinet security cluster (executive) and Congress (legislative).
5. Promoting BB to other potential partner stakeholders.
6. Institutionalizing the active partnership of government and civil society (Schirch and Mancini-Griffoli 2015: 103).

As a pioneering project, this locally based civil society initiative changed the relationship between societal actors and security providers. As shared by a civil society member,

> Military now plays a vital role as protector of the civilians. This lessened human rights violations because the military has learned that they have to connect with the community. Before, they were hard to get or they were very sensitive and defensive especially when we brought cases of rape [against soldiers] to the [meeting] sessions (Schirch and Macini-Griffoli 2015: 103).

a.4. Impact on SDG-16

There are no rigorous studies on the impact of civil society-led SSR initiatives on meeting the targets set by SDG-16. However, one could make the connection between projects such as BB which increases non-state civilian oversight to further inculcating principles of accountability, transparency, and participation that lie at the core of SDG-16. However, it could be surmised that the gains for SSR were largely due to several endogenous and exogenous factors of civil society such as its value-alignments with a democratic government, cordial relations with security forces, and the presence of a pro-liberal democracy government.

However, civil society's SSG/R achievements from 2010 to 2015 were disrupted with the rise to power of populist president Rodrigo Duterte in 2016. No president in the country's post-martial law history favored the military more than Duterte. It was not coincidental that once the firebrand leader decided to put his unconditional trust and confidence in the armed forces, this negatively affected Philippine democracy. As more and more members of the military (active or retired) fused themselves with the administration, it became more difficult to balance civil-military relations democratically. Some ex-generals in top cabinet posts even replaced left-leaning officials endorsed by the country's communist movement, a complete reversal of the more accommodating stance of the populist leader at the beginning of his presidency (Arugay 2021).

By 2017, the Duterte administration had the greatest number of retired generals in any presidential cabinet in the post-dictatorship period. Duterte appointed generals to head department portfolios that dealt with the environment and social welfare, the peace process and indigenous people's concerns, and several other smaller offices. This created an imbalance in civil-military relations and led to a slip toward securitized military-first policies on several fronts (Arugay 2023).

In the Philippines, this militarization of governance deprived policymaking of the plurality of perspectives necessary to contribute to addressing the complexity behind the country's security threats. Militarization pervaded bureaucracy as retired generals tapped into their existing military networks to lead their respective government agencies. It has been argued that this led to decision-makers prioritizing a very narrow range of responses. The lack of diverse perspectives in peace and security policy circles and an absence of debate on policy direction led to decision-makers favoring and actively seeking kinetic measures to respond to security challenges (Arugay et al. 2021).

In 2018, President Duterte signed an executive decree to 'end local communist armed conflict' by the end of his term in 2022. This unconditional order is believed to have been strongly influenced by the military establishment's enduring interest in taking advantage of the current administration's subservience to their goals. Euphemistically described as a 'whole of nation' approach, the heavily funded counter-insurgency strategy was largely dictated by elements of the military establishment. The Duterte administration's inability to impose democratic civilian control put the military 'in the driver's seat' in this anti-communist drive. With both retired and active generals leading on implementation, the military was determined to put a violent—rather than negotiated—end to one of the world's longest-running Maoist-inspired insurgencies. In recent months, President Duterte's administration accelerated a McCarthy-esque campaign against an insurgency that it saw as having penetrated all sectors of society. Historically viewed as rebels or political opposition, the communist movement is now labeled as a 'terrorist group' (Arugay 2023). Thus, under Duterte, not only was civil society's input missing, but there was a total reversal of how his government viewed civil society's role in SSG, from partners to enemies.

The gap left by civil society in security governance became an indication of the overall regression of democratic quality in the Philippines. In all metrics of democratic governance, the Philippines has been downgraded since 2016 as seen in Figure 1 below.

According to the Bertelsmann Transformation Index (BTI), the democratic status of the Philippines were downgraded from a 'defective democracy' in 2014 (left side of the figure) to a 'highly defective democracy' in 2022 (right side of the figure). One can also notice that the scores of the Philippines were reduced in all five indicators with the rule of law and stability of democratic institutions receiving the highest reduction in scores. This is empirical evidence of the existing accountability deficit in the country under the Duterte administration.[2]

It is therefore not surprising that the Philippines is not making steady progress in meeting SDG-16 targets. As seen in Figure 2, there are some indicators where the country has lagged and even stagnated. It can be noticed that two indicators—the Corruption Perception Index and the Press Freedom Index—indicated a downward trend for the Philippines. These are proxies for the state of transparency and accountability in each country. A 2021 study of Transparency International also found that the Philippines has a moderate risk for corruption:

> Institutional resilience to corruption is modest across the Philippines' defense institutions. Oversight of policymaking and procurement by parliament is particularly weak and transparency remains limited throughout the sector, including with regards to financial management.[3]

Civil society could have positively contributed to addressing these SSG deficits, but these negative assessments are consistent with the Philippines' state of civil society freedom and space. According to CIVICUS, the country currently has a repressed civil society under the Duterte administration,

---

[2]   More details about this assessment can be found at: https://bti-project.org/en/reports/country-report/PHL.
[3]   A more detailed report can be accessed here: https://ti-defence.org/gdi/countries/philippines/.

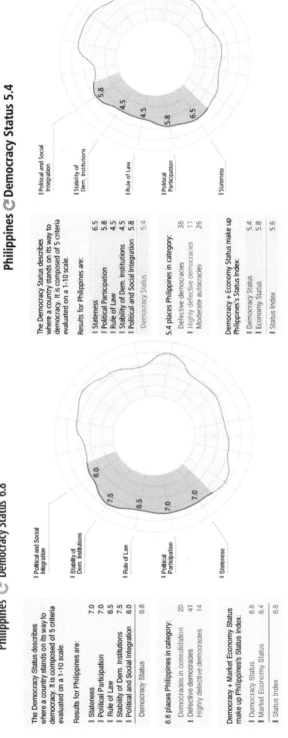

Figure 1: Democratic Regime Quality in the Philippines.

Source: Bertelsmann Transformation Index.

SDG16 – Peace, Justice and Strong Institutions

Homicides (per 100,000 population)	4.4 2019	●	↑
Unsentenced detainees (% of prison population)	59.2 2019	●	↗
Population who feel safe walking alone at night in the city or area where they live (%)	68 2021	◐	↑
Property Rights (worst 1–7 best)	4.4 2020	◐	↑
Birth registrations with civil authority (% of children under age 5)	91.8 2020	◐	●
Corruption Perception Index (worst 0–100 best)	33 2021	●	↓
Children involved in child labor (% of population aged 5 to 14)	NA NA	●	●
Exports of major conventional weapons (TIV constant million USD per 100,000 population)	0.0 2020	●	●
Press Freedom Index (best 0–100 worst)	45.6 2021	●	↓
Access to and affordability of justice (worst 0–1 best)	0.5 2020	●	↑

Figure 2: Philippine Performance in SDG-16 Indicators in 2021.[4]

given the shrinking civic space, targeted harassment of dissidents and journalists, a draconian anti-terror law, and digital repression of dissent.[5]

The Philippine case study reveals several points. Civil society's diversity, robustness and democratic character made it a powerful actor that could primarily promote accountability in governance, particularly in SSG. This endogenous condition was complemented by external factors such as a democratic regime an openness of security forces to partner with CSOs. The case of BB was illustrative of the ability of civil society to contribute to enhancing SSG by implementing SSR. This, in turn, had an important contribution in fostering accountability within Philippine political institutions mandated to provide peace and security.

The case of the Philippines revealed the important role of civil society in pushing for SSR and challenging the orthodox notion that security policy is simply the domain of the government and service providers. It also underscored the importance of local ownership, the political will of the leadership to undertake SSR, and the willingness to include civil society. In the end, the 'whole of nation' approach benefitted the government, military, and the communities. But the Philippine case also has a cautionary caveat. It showed that the momentum for SSG/R initiatives could be easily undermined if political leaders lack the appreciation of the importance of SSG/R principles as well as the vital role of civil society as an agent of democratic accountability and oversight. In the end, SSR was not the only casualty under Duterte's populist-authoritarian government, as the country's democracy and steady progress toward meeting SDGs, particularly SDG-16, were also negatively affected.

b. Civil society in Tunisia: toward becoming a space for security discourse

The case of Tunisia demonstrated the limitations of the impact of SSR to meeting the targets of SDG-16, given the precarious nature of its transition toward democracy, the diversity of its civil society, particularly with the presence of semi-democratic or undemocratic social organizations,

---

[4] Source: https://sdg-tracker.org/peace-justice.
[5] See https://monitor.civicus.org/country/philippines/ for more details.

and the continued tutelary powers of the military and the police as leftovers from the previous authoritarian regime. Given these factors, SSR efforts in Tunisia remain a challenge, though some CSOs are maintaining the course of reform.

b.1. Exogenous factors

On 17 December 2011 in the town of Sidi Bouzid, a fruit vendor harassed by local police immolated himself out of despair. The incident catalyzed a spontaneous wave of demonstrations against the dire economic situation in Tunisia, marked by high youth unemployment and economic stagnation. Despite his initial defiance, the military refused to crack down on demonstrators and within a month, the protest movement forced Ben Ali—ruler of Tunisia for 23 years—to flee the country.

Amnesty International explained: 'President Ben Ali's two decades in office have been marred by a continuing pattern of human rights violations, including arbitrary arrests and detentions, torture and other ill-treatment, unfair trials, harassment and intimidation of human rights defenders and curbs on freedom of expression and association' (Amnesty International 2007: 1). During this time, Tunisia was also very active in combatting terrorism and radical extremism, with the regime historically being antagonistic to religious expressions and influence in political life under a secular Arab nationalist ideology (Koplow 2011) The United States Department of State (2008) assessed the country to have been generally successful in stemming terrorist activity, although the Interior Ministry and internal security forces were a notorious power center that presided over the curtailment of many civil liberties.

The event—which came to be known as the Jasmine Revolution—ignited a broader series of uprisings throughout the Middle East and North Africa, sometimes referred to as the 'Arab Spring.' In 2012, Tunisia 'became the first Arab country in more than three decades to receive a ranking of 3 or better for political rights on the 7-point Freedom House scale (in which 1 is most free)' (Stepan and Linz 2013: 18). In the years that followed, the Arab Spring's promise of political transformation toward more liberal political environments failed to live up to its promises in places like Egypt, Syria, and Libya, but persisted in Tunisia despite some public dissatisfaction and deficits in attaining transitional justice for the previous regime's rights violations (Robbins 2015). In a national assessment of the state of civil society in Tunisia, Mnasri (2016: 63) noted that civil society in the country successfully negotiated for more participatory decision-making:

> Gaining expertise in the associative field has allowed civil society components to shift from a force of protest whose only concern was to stand in opposition to the ruling authorities into a force of pressure and suggestion that is actively involved in national issues of public concern. It has thus managed to transcend the classical role it used to play before the revolution as a counter-power that monitored and exerted pressure on the authorities, to assume, after the revolution, a new participatory role that involves taking initiatives and making suggestions.

b.2. Endogenous factors

Although Tunisia underwent democratic backsliding since 2019, the window of political liberalization between 2012 and 2018 provided the conducive exogenous environment for CSO participation in the SSR and SDG-16 implementation. Specifically, prior to 2019 Tunisia's level of state capacity was not dramatically shattered by the democratic transition unlike other countries in the Middle East, which allowed for normalized relations between civil society and the country's transitional government. The shift in 2012 from outright authoritarian rule to emerging democratic practices provided a favorable opportunity structure for groups to advance claims on the state, as well as for the state to proactively solicit civil society input as part of what was then a thrust to increase transparency and participation. Today, Tunisian politics has been overtaken by authoritarian rule, including the dissolution of its parliament, the repression of civil society, and executive attacks against the judiciary (Roht-Arriaza 2022). It is important to note, however, that the Tunisian case embodied not only the failure of civil society to exercise a watchdog role on the state, but also the infighting inherent within civil society.

The past decade has displayed many illustrative facets of civil society's nature as an arena of discourse rather than an unqualified mechanism for accountability and inclusivity. One the one hand, strong CSOs—local activists, unions, non-governmental organizations, media, and the broader public—have undoubtedly shifted security discourse to responsible SSG and peacebuilding approaches, at least in terms of ideal goals by the state. On the other hand, Tunisia also illustrated the highly contested dynamics within civil society. The Tunisian revolution also opened space for more radical groups to advocate for public policies that shrink rather than defend democratic space, while many former state employees formed civic associations that blocked security sector reform (SSR) in a way that made associative life reflect variegated private interests rather than public good per se. Both developments in support of and detrimental to conventional SSG/R and SDG-16 principles prompted serious discussion of the ontology of civil society as a space for alternative discourses—an arena which allowed for alternatives to state-centric concepts of security and peace, but also one where anti-democratic thoughts could percolate and be hijacked by social actors whose interests were tied to authoritarian legacies.

b.3. CSO roles

Civil society in Tunisia became an important space wherein the contours of security and development discourse in Tunisia were defined. CSOs in Tunisia continued to exert direct political pressure after the fall of Ben Ali, but one important development was the sudden explosion of levels of direct influence on policymaking by non-state actors during the transitional period from 2011 to 2014. When there was distrust that early transitional leaders and former affiliates of the Ali regime were tempering the revolutionary nature of the planned transition, civil society actors such as the Tunisian League for Human Rights, Tunisian General Labor Union, key jurists, and the Islamist Ennahda Movement were able to exact a concession which led to the creation of the 'Higher Authority for the Realization of the Objectives of the Revolution, Political Reform, and Democratic Transition', an 'ad hoc body... that served as a kind of consultative assembly, debating and approving legislation during a period when Tunisia's parliament has been dissolved' and included CSOs, professionals, experts, and unionists in its ranks (Human Rights Watch 2011: 1).

Tunisian authorities also prioritized the drafting of the country's post-authoritarian constitution rather than having general elections. Elections were held to constitute the National Constituent Assembly (NCA) which drafted the constitution, and representatives were again drawn from civil society such as Moncef Marzouki who became the NCA's placeholder president-founder of the National Committee for the Defense of Prisoners of Conscience, and Mustapha Ben Jafar who founded the Tunisian Human Rights League. The composition of Tunisia's political institutions at the time was ideologically disparate groups united by Ali's oppression, such as Islamist groups previously persecuted, as well as secular CSOs focusing on civil-political rights. Gluck and Brandt observed that 'inclusion, transparency, and consultation were lacking during the early stages of Tunisia's constitutional review but picked up after the NCA presented its first draft to the public in August 2012. Following publication of a second draft, the NCA launched a two-month outreach campaign that included public meetings in the NCA representatives' constituencies, hearings with interest groups, and television broadcasts of most NCA debates and proceedings' (Gluck and Brandt 2015).

The most critical reform was the broader political commitment of Tunisia toward political pluralism. The first was the relaxation of authoritarian restrictions on freedom of association formerly done through administrative control over the grant of authorization for civic associations. A 2011 Decree-Law ended this and only required notification to appropriate authorities, paving the road for the proliferation of some 18,000 civic associations and organizations in Tunisia which expanded not just in service-delivery functions in education, health, and community development, but were also seen in new frontiers such as government accountability and SSR (Mnasri 2016). Freedom House's (2022) country report on Tunisia noted that groups of various political philosophies were generally free to form and operate, although there were acute deficiencies with respect to media freedom, exemptions to government transparency under security-related issues, and a 2018 law that effectively equated NGOs with businesses along with concomitant registration requirements.

First, with respect to SDG-16, Tunisian civil society was able to lobby the government for three things: (a) the specific usage of human rights discourse in national SDG16 targets and indicators; (b) developed specific targets for participatory decision-making (vaguely defined by UN itself) including targets to incorporate civil society in government decision-making; and (c) a 'right to information' target under SDG 16.10 to concretize how institutions could be made accountable (Laberge and Touihri 2019). More critically, CSOs in Tunisia successfully pushed for public perception surveys in measuring governance success that led to the government's 2017 Citizen Perceptions Towards Security, Freedom, and Local Governance. As argued in the framework of this paper, these successes were attributable to the favorable exogenous environment for civil society in Tunisia, which prior to 2019 was caught up in initial efforts by the post-Ben Ali governments to democratize. At the same time, as discussed above, Tunisian civil society had strained relations with the country's security providers, most notably because internal security forces mobilized sympathetic civil society groups to shield the police from transitional justice. In terms of the endogenous factors affecting civil society's overall strength, Tunisia had a fragmented civil society where pro-democratic forces did not have preponderance over non-democratic elements, which also naturally led to a split in values among CSOs.

Second, however, is that CSOs kept the democratization process going despite initial roadblocks, not least of which was the infighting between political parties who disagreed over the content of the constitution. Salafists advocated Sharia-inspired constitutionalism, while secular groups pushed for provisions generally in line with liberal democracy. CSOs in Tunisia actively brokered the conclusion of the drafting of the new constitution in 2014, after an impasse in the first three years due to disagreements among political parties.

After an impasse in those first three years of the drafting of the new constitution, the Dialogue Quartet brokered political forces under a roadmap which included a caretaker technocratic government and a temporary step-down of the Islamist Ennahda party which had come to power as a potent political force after the Jasmine Revolution. Amid polarized public rhetoric pertaining to competing secular and faith-based visions for the constitution, the National Dialogue Quartet stepped in to ensure progress toward a pluralistic-liberal political system. The Quartet was composed of the Tunisian General Labor Union (UGTT), Tunisian Confederation of Industry, Trade, and Handicrafts (UTICA), Tunisian Human Rights League (LTDH), and the Tunisian Order of Lawyers, and was awarded the Nobel Peace Prize in 2015.

Other broad political changes included an effort to introduce SSR in Tunisia at the request of the Ministry of the Interior, as well as the constitutional provision for participatory democracy and open governance in the implementation of development programs. While reality often fell short of these expectations, the discursive shift toward greater political role by civil society was undeniable. Chaker writes that civil society 'successfully pushed consecutive governments to adopt the laws necessary to advance human rights, such as the 2013 Law on Transitional Justice, the 2017 Law for the Elimination of Violence Against Women, and the 2018 Law Against Racial

Discrimination', although conservatism and entrenched practices remain strong in Tunisian society (Chaker 2021: 1).

This, in effect, set a baseline and approximate direction from which reforms would take place and crowded out other ideas also present in civil society at the time, such as a restoration of the status quo. It is worth underscoring that some civil society actors at the time actively frustrated movements toward liberal-democratic aspirations. In the case of Tunisia's SSR, former members of the police forces—many of whom were dismissed or resigned from security forces after the revolution—formed security professionals' associations such as the National Union of Internal Security forces and the Federation of Unions of Internal Security Forces. Both advocated to shield security personnel from accountability in the multi-sectoral stakeholder meetings undertaken to reform the internal security apparatus from its authoritarian legacy of extensive human rights violations, as well as being a deliberate strategy to dilute the SSR agenda to focus on training, internal oversight, and capability-building (Kartas 2014). Unions sympathetic to security forces came to commission meetings and openly confronted former victims and tried to explain a defense discourse to the public. This strategy had substantial gains primarily because high levels of transitional political instability and public anxiety stemmed from the behavior of non-state groups, especially armed Salafists, and the many self-proclaimed leagues to 'protect the revolution.'

b.4. Impact on SDG-16

Tunisia's SSR agenda focused on three broad areas—professionalization and readiness, counterterrorism, and border security—although assessments agree that there was a mixed record, especially on the more political nature of transitional justice issues and human rights accountability; these were diluted by pro-security unions in favor of the 'train and equip' style of international security sector assistance, mostly because the post-2014 global strategic environment was then confronting the Islamic State and rise in radical extremism (Shah and Dalton 2020).

This is not to say that SSR was a failure in Tunisia, as there were remarkable gains especially from the baseline of open authoritarianism. SSR programs also included soft projects, including among these dialogue, community policy, and local security council arrangements. The balance between both hard and soft approaches, which were unevenly supported by non-state groups with different interests, reflects both the heterogeneity of voices and balance of forces within civil society. The case of Tunisia shows the nature of civil society as an arena of contending visions. For this reason, there were also major efforts at the programming level to reconcile various social interests, particularly around Local Security Councils, which were spaces where 'often-opposed actors ... can sit together, talk, and identify problems,' recognizing that many groups were in fact themselves concerned about the effective provision of security, due to rising urban everyday violence rather than just institutional reforms on the police and security forces (Haugbølle and Chemlali 2019: 1).

Between the brief democratic opening from 2012 to 2018, DCAF (2017) assessed that:

- There was improvement in transparency in Tunisia's security and justice sectors. There was a systematic effort to publish laws, decree-laws, decrees, and circulars which picked up in 2016–2017.
- In addition to this, there were indicators of the dividends of these reforms. For one thing, the first youth organization working specifically on SSR—Le Réseau Alternatif des Jeunes or RAJ—was the only youth organization that publicly came out against a controversial draft law on offenses against armed forces.

- Also, the Ministry of Interior's communication channels toward media, which was previously neglected and used only as an extension of propaganda work, gradually improved toward more professional and transparent relations with journalists. However, progress has not been symmetrical: there had been progress relating to rule of law, gender equality, human rights, and media freedom but there was less success in terms of improve the weak regulations on the use of force, the structure of the police and intelligence services, and a general minimal movement for oversight and accountability in the security sector.

There are several observations worth noting in Tunisia's civil society as a space for discourse. First, civil society was not an unconditional supporter of democracy and SSR. This is consistent with prior literature that warns of the 'uncivil' elements in the non-state sector. Part of the reason for this is that the usual orientations of CSOs normally tapped as development partners for SSG/R or peacebuilding projects did not necessarily represent the majority opinion or hegemonic ideas in a society. Hitherto undiscussed differences in interests and values in civil society came to the fore when they started participating in national politics, as was evident in counter-demonstrations relating to human rights and legislation specifically on women empowerment, particularly when some Ennahda representatives even proposed using Sharia as the source of Tunisian law in 2012 (Deane 2013).

The country continuously experienced Islamist-secular political polarization concomitant with the liberalized political space, including social groups that had anti-democratic, anti-liberal orientations. It is worth noting that the dominant civil society groups in Tunisia—such as those that formed the Quartet—existed even during the authoritarian regime and were highly focused on sectoral concerns and service-delivery to constituents rather than a broader political transformation agenda. This was partly the reason that network creation was so utilized by CSOs under the SDGs, as it could provide a means to move CSOs beyond sectoral concerns and to advance broader agendas. The critical differences in the composition and nature of organizations in civil society determined its ability to effectively aggregate social demands for civil political action and influence.

Second, some even credit the success of brokerage by these CSOs in preventing a downward spiral of conflict during constitutional discussions to their perceived political mediation. This is consistent with case studies in Afghanistan that in weak-state contexts, civil society positions itself as neutral, simultaneously both reducing collaboration with government and local armed actors, while still dealing with both (CIVIC 2017a; Schmeidl 2009). There is a gap in the literature on the extent to which mainstream SSG/R and SDG efforts integrate this perspective at the programmatic level, but it is also typical to find international development support for inherently pro-state projects relating to PCVE, for example.

Third, because SDG-16 contains various concepts on good governance and security which have different operational end goals—such as those in SDG-16A on combatting crime and terrorism and those relating to targets on participatory decision-making (16.7) and creating accountable institutions (16.6)—these principles sometimes conflict in a way that tests civil society, but also sometimes allows them to shape the local discourse around CSOs and their relevance to the broader peacebuilding efforts in a country. Tunisia was under great pressure to bring local AML/CFT regulations in line with global standards after being put into both FATF and EU blacklists. CSOs in Tunisia 'felt the squeeze' in terms of operational space. The response of civil society was to convene CSOs to participate in developing the Risk Assessment of the sector and relay findings and secure buy-in from the Financial Intelligence Unit of Tunisia (the Commission Tunisienne des Analyses Financières). They successfully proposed a new methodology for the assessment, as well as securing their participation in the process. In 2019, Tunisia was one of only six countries rated to be compliant with FATF's new Recommendation 8 to protect civil society and mitigate downstream harms of AML/TF regulations, namely bank de-risking, CSO registration, and transactions of due diligence that imposed substantial administrative costs to operate an organization.

Finally, it is also worth noting that the BTI country report on Tunisia reported that most Tunisians remained unlikely to volunteer their time for CSOs, reflecting low social capital (Bertelsmann Stiftung 2022). The BTI report also notes that Afrobarometer data from 2018 indicate that four in five Tunisians do did not feel affinity to a major political party, complicating coalition-building in society. The conflict between the Islamist Ennahda party and the secularist Free Destourian Party (PDL), formed by many pre-revolution authoritarian elites, reflected broader disagreements and norm contestations that permeated both civil and political spheres. A paramount practical consideration in this regard was how to push SDG-16 and SSR—which are theoretically informed by liberal-democratic values—in highly polarized contexts where the precepts of those reforms are under debate. The question then is to what extent can reform ideals truly be locally owned? Are CSOs relegated to service-delivery and project-implementer roles in SDG-16 and SSR projects precisely because their values are already assumed a priori as universally desirable and necessary? In foreign donor-driven contexts, are there downstream political consequences when the impulse is to immediately roll out SSR and SDG-16 development projects, regardless of the actual acceptability and level of support for these ideas, or the hope that buy-in can be secured during project implementation and not before it? These are important questions to ask moving forward. Torres (2021: 14) observes that there must be more attention to the struggle of ideas within civil society descriptions that no longer fit the 'heroic narrative' of civil society, to better address the issue of growing political polarization and the practical problems that ensue from it:

> While civil society historically has often been an engine of democratic change, in each of these struggles there was a sector of civil society that stood on the other side of the same issues. In an era of increased mobilization, but also of dubious commitments to democracy and human rights, it is important not to make blanket assumptions about the character of civil society. All protests are also not necessarily promoting progressive or pro-democratic goals, but nativists, chauvinists, supremacists, and others with exclusionary agendas are just as able to use civil disobedience to advance their aims. Polarization is growing in civil society, as in politics. With growing polarization, people are more likely to cling to their sense of group identity and to regard their own group as under siege, compelling them to rise collectively.

c. Civil society in Somalia: the pursuit of alternative security provision

The case of Somalia exposes the hybridity of security provision which is a reality in most fragile or conflict-ridden societies. In this country, regime and state capacity was at its weakest which made it difficult for state security forces to assert control over the land. Certain organizations from civil society filled this gap by providing security as a public good in their community. This veered away from the conventional roles accorded to civil society in SSG, and it is still not certain how they impact meeting SDG targets, given that Somalia has a poor record in SDG implementation. At best, this role of civil society does not fulfill the usual expectations toward their positive contributions and should be seen as a temporary stop-gap function while state-building is ongoing.

Various peacebuilding projects in the developing world have largely ignored the notion of civil society and private groups therein as alternative security providers—this led, for example, to the exclusion of non-state security and justice providers in conversations about the security family that needed to be reformed in SSG/R (Ghimire 2019). In cases where civil society groups were enjoined to participate, some peacebuilding projects were at risk of instrumentalization or being utilized by the state as project implementers within a broader state-centric ensemble of security activities (e.g., PCVE); however, in some cases, there was a lack of profound reflection on the potential of unintended consequences when civil society became the dominant humanitarian aid provider and human security patron in weak state contexts (Suri 2016).

c.1. Exogenous factors

In the case of Somalia, the insurgent Islamist group Harakat al-Shabaab al-Mujahdeen (al-Shabaab) has firmly established itself as of this writing in the southern and central parts of the country, and controls major supply routes and exercises congruent state-like functions on taxation and judicial administration. Dovetailing the global war on terror, Somalia's federal government was extensively supported by the international community to the tune of USD 1.5 billion each year; roughly 8 out of 10 federal employees were employed within the security sector (World Bank 2020). The country was an example of a fragile or weak state, having collapsed in the 1990s and compounded by continuous social conflict and violence for much of its post-independence history. Somalia's security forces were a mixture of the Somalia National Army and the international coalition under the African Union Mission in Somalia (AMISOM), which was given a new mandate in April 2022 to take a more offensive posture against al-Shabaab. The central issue in Somalia was that civil society was torn between abuse and corruption-prone actors:

> All parties to the conflict in Somalia committed violations of international humanitarian law, some amounting to war crimes. The Islamist armed group Al-Shabab conducted indiscriminate and targeted attacks on civilians and forcibly recruited children. Inter-clan and intra-security force violence killed, injured, and displaced civilians, as did sporadic military operations against Al-Shabab by Somali government forces, troops from the African Union Mission in Somalia, and other foreign forces (Human Rights Watch 2021: 1).

Despite years of SSR and internationally funded peacebuilding projects, there remain remained key failures at the legal-policy level on initiatives intended for the creation of a national human rights commission and the revision of the country's outdated penal code. The federal government exerts exerted only limited authority beyond the capital of Mogadishu, with (in)security in most states maintained by state-based ethnic militias and the al-Shabaab. Political violence between actors is was common, with elections being marked by fraud and street-shootings in Mogadishu, as well as a contest between the Prime Minister Mohamed Roble and President Mohamed Abdullahi Mohamed over control of the National Intelligence and Security Agency (NISA). On the ground, clans maintain maintained private security networks as well as mediate among themselves for social, economic, and legal disputes. In contrast with the federal government, al-Shabaab has made inroads in de facto controlling major swathes of territory by working through these alternative governance mechanisms.

To be sure, there was substantial progress in the Somali SSR, although this was mostly technical in nature, relating to payroll reform and force training rather than ambitious political transformation projects, primarily because the strategic situation demanded a first-order prioritization to build up state capacity (Africa Center for Strategic Studies 2018). SSG/R in Somalia followed the typical UN model of development aid wherein donor states funded the deployment of technical experts on critical peace and security functions, institutionalized international humanitarian law (IHL) and international human rights law (IHRL), and contributed a significant portion of the de facto security forces in the country under AMISOM. At the same time, there were criticisms of the apparent futility of building a centralized, Weberian state inherent in the SSG/R frameworks in fragile state contexts where the very multiplicity of security providers—state and non-state—were a fact of life and would change only once broader economic, demographic, and political factors enable state formation (Menkhaus 2016).

Relatedly, the monitoring of SDG-16 targets in Somalia was also extremely difficult given serious state weakness, with no data available on homicides, perceptions on the protection of property rights, percentage of children involved in labor, and access to justice.[6] Many CSOs operated in Somalia to advance SDG-16 goals and formed a regional SDG16+ Coalition to coordinate action. The Somali Institute for Development Research and Analysis noted that, in practice, CSOs directly delivered vital public services such as social protection programs and infrastructure needed to meet societal needs, aside from the traditional role of civil society helping the government to localize SDG-16 initiatives by raising awareness, conducting research, engaging the grassroots, and putting forth recommendations for state planning (Somali Institute for Development Research and Analysis 2019).

Despite these, no less than the UN Mission in Somalia prudently pointed out that such efforts 'have been met with only limited success for many reasons, including fighting an ongoing insurgency while trying to reform, a lack of capacity within the institutions, a lack of coordination by donors and partners, and the lack of a coherent government security policy.' There were notable gains though, such as the fact that 'the number of casualties attributed to the Somali National Army and Police, as well as AMISOM, was significantly smaller than those attributed to al-Shabaab militants' (UN Assistance Mission in Somalia 2017: 9).

There were also humanitarian groups operating in Somalia that operated across entire communities because of their distribution of aid, immediate security for target communities, and mediation with al-Shabaab to allow for these resources to flow into conflict zones and rebel-held areas. Saferworld observed that because of their importance in the livelihood of local people, regional actors pressured humanitarian groups to withhold aid to terrorist-controlled areas for fear that such donations fueled conflict since they ended up in the hands of armed actors (Suri 2016). On the other hand, other works on how NGOs played it safe in conflict zones also led to inefficient allocation of peace and development aid because civil society would only focus efforts on urban areas where the security situation was more manageable, rather than in rural violence-prone communities that had greater need for humanitarian aid. The dilemma in the abovementioned scenarios stemmed from the reality that in the absence of the state, civil society became a primary security provider.

c.2. Endogenous factors

Some Somali CSOs and clan-based institutions operated in areas controlled by al-Shabaab and maintained a low profile, often performing functions such as delivering social services and mediating between clan conflicts (UN Assistance Mission in Somalia 2017). In addition to this, because of the large power vacuum in the country, many of the programs on DDR, trauma healing, and transitional justice were directly provided by civil society without a concomitant official channel or centralized program from the government (Felbab-Brown 2018). One report pointed out that those few organizations that chose to continue engagement were argued to benefit from areas such as gaining more accurate assessment of key grievances from insurgents, opening space for the consideration of 'alternative views of contested issues and history,' and providing opportunities for constructive exchange that increased the overall capacity and probability of dialogue (Lederach et al. 2011: 12).

Civil society and civilians, however, were 'not merely pawns in the interaction between governments and rebel groups in civil conflicts, they have some autonomy in expressing demands for services provided by either side' of combatants (Life & Peace Institute 2014: 37). This was evident in the subject of the mediation of civil society between insurgents and governments to advance

---

[6] See Sustainable Development Report 2022 and Somalia's country profile at https://dashboards.sdgindex.org/.

civil protection and harm mitigation. Aside from Somalia, Afghan communities had several coping strategies to engage armed actors to increase their safety. First, they attempted to normalize relations with these armed groups if government presence was weak to reduce harm and violence to civilians. Second, they positioned themselves as neutral (e.g., reducing collaboration with government) to avoid retaliatory attacks by armed groups. Third, they crafted agreements in secret for armed groups to not operate in their areas to prevent counterattacks (CIVIC 2017b). CIVIC's research showed that CSOs and community leaders were eager to directly engage armed actors to have quick redress for everyday concerns such as indiscriminate violence and abuse by armed combatants, and to lobby for humanitarian corridors. This behavior, unsurprisingly, was motivated by the situation where civil society operated in a scenario where there was a tremendous security vacuum and thus had to operate as an actor in its own right, although security provision necessarily entailed other conventional functions such as the monitoring of combatants (watchdog) and active brokerage of security and development discourse.

c.3. CSO roles

In the case of Somalia, the core of civil society was not non-government organizations, professional associations, or the media, but rather clan structures, led by elders who directly negotiated between armed actors, sought to advance community interests, and had at times competing interests that altogether muddled the notion of a singular civil society voice for major issues. These community-based or indigenous structures were organic to Somalia and, as discussed in the Literature Review, reflected inherent power asymmetries and customs that might not necessarily fit the traditional expectations of 'civil society.' According to Osman (2018:1):

> There are numerous experiences of outside supporters of Somalia CSOs becoming frustrated because local CSO partners turned out to be politically biased or unreliable, primarily serving the interests of their beneficiaries and at times favorite political groups or even being as ruthless as the governments they are supposed to counterbalance... Clan affiliations are strong in Somalia, manifesting through different institutions and even within civil society. For example, some diaspora-funded NGOs are established along clan lines and mainly run projects in areas to which certain families can trace back their lineages. This is hardly surprising. For many CSOs that attempt to cut across clan lines and bring about positive change, clan politics can get in the way. Because of this reality, many CSOs cannot escape becoming aligned with one group or another, either in reality or in perception. Somali CSOs are often seen as either supporting the state administration or the opposition party or clan, depending on who is leading the organization at the time. This is especially true when the government engages on politically sensitive topics, such as elections, boundaries, clan disputes, or resource sharing.

Based on the types of SSR approaches, (Table 1), this situation of civil society being a direct security provider such as in Somalia occurred in situations where the dominant peacebuilding and security reform approach was that of stabilization. Under the two other approaches—the 'train and build' and 'orthodox SSR' approaches—there is a functional state that acts as the center of gravity for reform efforts, which inevitably defines the role of civil society in peacebuilding in conventional Weberian state-society relations. While civilian protection mechanisms such as dialogues with government and rebel forces and the monitoring of civilian harm fall within the usual watchdog and accountability function of civil society, in practice CSOs became duty-bearers to functions traditionally performed by the state, especially in the administration of justice and provision of security services. In so doing, the expanded role for civil society and other private actors delayed or hampered the emergence of normal Weberian state-society relations.

c.4. Impact on SDG-16

Other countries such as Burkina Faso, Mali, and Nigeria share some similarities with Somalia. Some communities in these countries responded to violent environments like banditry or insurgency by establishing parallel defense groups, which themselves became heavily armed over time and could become a source of violence against civilians; these became magnets for violence and were seen more as a necessary evil rather an unconditional guarantor of peace (Catholic Relief Services 2019). These contexts and the conceptual grayness of 'civil' society as a concept in conflict-affected environments are important in interrogating the concept in SSG/R and SDG-16 which tends to assume that civil society functions are neatly demarcated from state services and can be compartmentalized as a partner of an essentially state-based program, or that the state has a monopoly of violence or power of command vis-a-vis these non-state actors. There are no easy answers and hard-and-fast rules in developing a framework for CSO integration in SSR/G and SDG-16; as Jackson notes, the more productive issue then is not just focusing on what the goals of these programs are, but to examine 'what it means to carry [them] out' (Jackson in Sedra 2010: 21).

The centrality of civil society and private groups in steering political decisions in conflict-affected zones could be problematic especially since leadership structures could be undemocratic or merely reflect pre-existing power dynamics. For this reason, there are also arguments that civil society's place in peacebuilding and security reform as watchdogs should not be assumed, since in several instances these non-state groups are also properly the subject of what needs to be transformed. For Ghimire, building infrastructures of peace thus requires both horizontal integration between civil society actors, and vertical integration with the state (Ghimire 2019). Somalia's case indicated a strong slant for vertical integration of civil society in the SSG/R and SDG-16 initiatives, to the point that sometimes such programs risked instrumentalizing civil society as an extension of state activities. At the same time, conventional policy on global counterterrorism for example had not come to grips with the reality of security co-provision by civil society and the reality on the ground of their transactions with armed actors to avoid civilian harm (Saferworld 2019).

In fragile and conflict-affected countries such as Somalia, the weakness of the state and the centrality of non-state actors in security provision and decision-making that had significant bearing on conflict also pointed to the possibility that civil society itself was a legitimate object of SSG, although broader peacebuilding was ignored in mainstream development strategies. Issues such as ethnic discrimination and the supremacy of kinship ties over civic identity in politics were often conflict drivers, as well as barriers to an inclusive and participative security sector; these were broader issues which were not just resolved through technical capacity-building, but broader, more transformative liberal peacebuilding (Krause and Jutersonke 2005). At the same time, this outlook entailed questions relating how to achieve a civil society that had the structural preconditions to prevent intra-societal violence and animosities, and whether this should be part of the broader SSG/R and SDG-16 agenda. Nonetheless, there was no denying that highly political issues of economic distribution, culture, customs, and power relations within civil society fueled conflict patterns and prospects of attaining sustainable peace. In contrast, studies with relatively moderate or nascent effective state presence listed more generic concerns on civil-military relations, such as civilian control over instruments and organizations of lethal force, rule of law, and capacity-building of state security providers such as police or the army (Beeson et al. 2006; Sombatpoonsiri 2018). The problem, Burt (2016) argues, is that SSR and SDG-16 programs suffered from 'projectism' or smaller-scale, easily implementable programs that were capable of quick-wins by targeting familiar state-based institutions and reform laundry lists (Burt 2016).

To an extent, there is truth in criticisms which say that security and development discourses have not adequately considered the direct role played by civil society in contexts where it had to step up to fill a security gap. At the surface level, although the case of Somalia enlarged the participation of different stakeholders in security provision, there were also limitations in this

implementation of this role in meeting SDG-16 targets. The key factors suggested that the autonomy of civil society from other coercive actors and those who held political power was severely
limited. This deprived the ability of CSOs to contribute toward SDG-16 implementation.

As this section has argued, the reality is often messy at the operational level: CSOs are able
to better secure the conscious effort by combatants to minimize or avoid civilian harm in ways
when they act as local power brokers, but at the same time there are concerns about the potential
reprisal on such groups and its members if they become perceived as supporting terrorism and
insurgency. There is no denying that CSOs could be channels by which the 2030 Agenda, SDG-
16, and SSG/R could be advanced and implemented; however, their embeddedness in political,
economic, and social structures in their respective countries and the dilemmas posed by this also
emphasize the point that they too are part of the scope of reform and not just its implementers. It
also cannot be discounted that the larger the direct security role played by civil society, the less
it becomes 'civil society' conventionally defined and behaving more like shadow state institutions.

CHAPTER V

Conclusions & Policy Recommendations

The concluding chapter summarizes the main arguments and findings of this paper. It also contains several policy recommendations for donors, external actors, states, security sector institutions, and civil society actors.

a. Main findings

This paper discussed the various roles played by civil society and its multiple organizational forms in the pursuit of SSG/R and SDG-16. It argued that civil society has played various roles in promoting SSG/R around the world. While they are often accorded limited and secondary status to states and external actors, CSOs serve important roles in realizing the aims of SSG/R. Civil society's propensity to focus on human security issues and democratic governance issues could serve as a useful intermediary in linking the SSG/R and SDG-16 discourses because of civil society's emphasis on good governance principles such as accountability, transparency, and participation. As both discourses seek to decenter the focus on state and sovereign power, civil society is equipped and willing, and has the legitimacy to pursue the reform of the security sector as well as contribute to the fulfillment of SDGs.

SSG/R and SDG-16 are change-oriented paradigms that are linked by the centrality of human security in development planning by focusing on individual needs in economic, health, environmental, personal, community, and political spheres. Consequently, they expand the focus of security assistance in development and aid policy thinking by drawing attention to non-traditional concerns relating to structural rather than merely direct violence which threatens the survival, livelihood, and dignity of people. Relating SSG/R and SDG-16 reinforces the idea that security and development are intertwined and mutually reinforcing.

How to cite this book chapter:
Arugay, A. A. & Baquisal, J. K. A. 2024. *Accountability, Discourse, and Service Provision: Civil Society's Roles in Security Sector Governance and Reform (SSG/R) and Sustainable Development Goal-16 (SDG-16).* Pp. 55–60. London: Ubiquity Press. DOI: https://doi.org/10.5334/bcy.e. License: CC-BY-NC

This paper argued that civil society's capacity to contribute to SSG/R depends on the interplay between endogenous and exogenous factors. The former refers to civil society's structural composition and value orientation, while the latter concerns the country's particular regime type, its state capacity, and the relationship between civil society and security providers. There is no single factor that determines the success of civil society in promoting SSG/R, but these factors form the environment in which civil society could play an active role in influencing SSG/R initiatives. This paper found that a bigger, diverse, more pluralistic, and democratic civil society has the potential to contribute to SSR. Moreover, a more democratic regime, a well-capacitated state, and cordial relations between civil society and security providers are elements of an external environment conducive to civil society involvement in SSG/R. Each country has a unique combination of factors that are exogenous and endogenous to civil society, and that will impact its SSG/R process and by extension the implementation of SDG-16 targets. This paper argued that successful SSR pursued by civil society could meet a few of the objectives of SDG-16 such as accountability, transparency, and participation. In this case, there is almost a complete overlap between SSG/R and SDG-16. Given that this paper is the first attempt to link civil society's role in SSG/R and SDG-16, there are still unexplored areas between the two that could be done by future research. Such studies could systematically examine the causal relationship between civil society efforts in meeting the objectives of these two discourses of change.

The first role as an agent of oversight and accountability was seen in the case of the Philippines from 2010 to 2016 where CSOs became an agent of democratic accountability and oversight to the country's security providers, particularly the military. The *BB* initiative enabled civil society to become a 'watchdog' by monitoring the implementation of the AFP's main internal security strategy. This was due to civil society's enduring advocacy of good governance and accountability that was consistent with the political leadership's orientation during that time. However, the Philippine case also showed that gains from civil society participation could also be quickly undermined by a new government which not only had disdain for civil society but was also bent on eroding democratic principles. Under Duterte's populist-authoritarian rule, there was a strained state-civil society relationship that not only put a stop to the SSR process but also weakened the ability of the government to meet SDG targets, including those that were relevant to SDG-16.

This paper also examined two other roles played by civil society in SSG/R. Apart from overseeing security forces and institutions, emergent roles put CSOs as an important space for security discourse, especially in countries where SSG/R programming was heavily driven by state actors. This was another new role for civil society, found in fragile states and countries where the security had effectively broken down.

Civil society in Tunisia became an important space for security and development discourses. Its strong CSOs—local activists, unions, non-governmental organizations, media, and the broader public—undoubtedly shifted security discourse to responsible SSG and peacebuilding approaches. To their credit, CSOs kept the democratization process going despite initial roadblocks, not least of which was the infighting between political parties who disagreed over the content of the constitution. CSOs in Tunisia actively brokered the conclusion of the drafting of the new constitution in 2014, but an important aspect to this occurrence was the a priori existence of such networks in the country, as well as the generally manageable security situation in the country. This, in effect, set a baseline and approximate direction from which more security and development reforms would take place, and crowded out other ideas also present in civil society at the time, such as a restoration of status quo. In other words, Tunisian civil society shaped the security-development discourse that would influence more reform initiatives in the country. This, perhaps, was the reason why Tunisia was strides in fulfilling its SDG-16 targets despite still being in a process of political transition. But Tunisia also illustrated the highly contested dynamics within civil society that pointed to the non-automaticity of the linkage between civil society activity and SSR and SDG-16 success. The Tunisian revolution opened space for more radical groups to advocate for public policies that shrank rather than defended democratic space, while many former state employees formed civic associations that blocked SSR.

The case studies for the third role of CSOs which is as an alternative security provider focused on fragile and conflict-affected states such as Somalia. SDG-16 and SSR were particularly difficult to implement in such contexts, primarily because the issue was about the security and power vacuum rather than reorienting security and justice mechanisms that in practice did not frequently reach large segments of the population. Within this environment, civil society's role became heightened—from providing social services to becoming actors that brokered between the state and threat elements. It must be noted that this security provision role was considered as a 'gray zone' for civil society: Firstly, they attempted to normalize relations with armed groups if government presence was too weak to reduce harm and violence to civilians. In some cases, they ceased to become civil society if non-state actors took it upon themselves to provide for the defense of their communities. These exigencies were arguably not sufficiently accounted for in SSR and SDG-16 frameworks which primarily operate on the assumption that civil society takes a more secondary role to the state, such as by joining mechanisms, providing research, or being a watchdog of the government.

Second, they positioned themselves as neutral (e.g., reducing collaboration with government) to avoid retaliatory attacks by armed groups. Third, they crafted agreements in secret for armed groups to not operate in their areas to prevent counterattacks. CSOs became duty-bearers to functions traditionally performed by the state, especially in the administration of justice and provision of security services. In so doing, the expanded role for civil society and other private actors delayed or hampered the emergence of normal Weberian state-society relations. In establishing parallel defense groups, which themselves became heavily armed over time and could become a source violence against civilians, these became 'magnets for violence' and were seen more as a necessary evil rather than an unconditional guarantor of peace. The dilemmas inherent in this role of civil society as an alternative security provider were discussed in this paper, and how they were informed by and affected SDG-16 and SSR. More research is needed in how this role is implemented, given their implications for the integrity of social organizations as civil actors distinct from the state. If CSOs are successful in providing this role, how can this be reconciled with the duty of the state as the main security provider within society? How is this different with the privatization of security carried out by for-profit entities? All these questions limit the paper's ability to effectively evaluate this emergent role. Thus, these sets of findings must not be construed as an approval of this role.

The findings of the case studies must be understood given the paper's limitations of being unable to wholistically analyze the entire set of factors that could explain the ability of CSOs to contribute to SSG/R and by extension, some targets of SDG-16. As the logic of comparison was purposive, it did not control for the comparability of the three case countries. Future research could systematically conduct comparison of case countries that have more similar contexts, and perhaps more comparisons within regions could be done, given their possible similarity in contexts and other explanatory conditions. As this paper is the first of its kind to engage this topic, part of the research agenda in the future would be to investigate more systematically how CSOs perform these three roles and possibly other roles that could contribute to SSG/R and SDG-16.

b. Policy recommendations

This paper provides several policy recommendations for the effective and inclusive engagement of civil society in both SSG/R and SDG-16.

1. For external actors (international institutions and foreign donors)
   a. *Treat civil society as a serious actor in SSG/R and SDG16.* International institutions and foreign donors should view civil society as a serious partner in both change-oriented paradigms. It should not be an afterthought or be invited to provide legitimacy to

existing state or institutional initiatives. This entails continuous involvement, iterative consultations, and meaningful integration of its inputs and contributions to SSG/R and SDG-16. While it may cost more time, resources, and energy, this paper showed that in general, there is always merit in including civil society in the process.

b. *Recognize the diversity and dynamism of civil society.* As governments change, so does the make-up and composition of civil society. International institutions and foreign donors must view civil society not as a monolithic entity and must better account for this reality in the very inception of project frameworks. They could provide the venues to reconcile oftentimes conflicting voices within civil society by establishing consultative mechanisms that are inclusive in nature. There is a perception among security practitioners that expanding the number of actors involved satisfies inclusivity but also potentially makes programs vulnerable to spoilers. This fear, however, must not compromise the principles of inclusive participation that are inherent in both SSG/R and SDG-16.

c. *Integrate SDGs in SSG/R programming.* Given that both SSG/R and the SDGs are frameworks created and/or embraced by the United Nations, there is a need to integrate them in the frameworks of international organizations and the donor community. This paper showed that at the present, there could be more efforts to have clearer and direct linkages between the two discourses of change. The security sector comprises a considerable part of the state apparatus and society. Thus, SDG implementation could truly benefit from successful SSR. International organizations could ask countries to report SSR efforts in SDG implementation. On the other hand, donors supporting SSR could also integrate SDG implementation, especially if they provide support to governments, security forces, and equally important, to CSOs.

d. *Understand the politicized environment of civil society advocacy.* Oftentimes, external actors avoid directly dealing with civil society actors deemed as more political than others, given that some CSOs are engaged in larger political struggles against the state. This 'impartial' stance makes SSG/R and SDG interventions seemingly apolitical and technical. However, it is already established that SSR processes are political in nature. In this regard, being impartial does not mean that external actors are not able to intervene when civil society is being repressed, threatened, and undermined by their governments in the conduct of their SSR activities. This is a sensitive topic that could be further discussed among relevant external actors dealing with SSG/R and SDG interventions in another country. Thus, having a unified, coherent, and common strategy in dealing with civil society is important.

2. For states and security providers
   a. *Include civil society in SSG/R assessment and planning.* It is assumed that CSOs are often willing to engage the state in undertaking reforms. However, they should be included not only in the middle of the process or as an afterthought. Civil society participation starts at the beginning of the SSR process, which is the assessment or evaluation phase that is followed by planning the reform process. States should adopt more inclusionary ways to foster civil society participation, including making sure that stakeholders are well represented. An example would be to include civil society in the formulation, implementation, and evaluation of meeting the goals of security or defense white papers or plans.

   b. *Adopt a consistent reform orientation to maintain trust.* Governments must ensure that SSG/R is not seen as an isolated reform effort detached from other governance reforms. Given that there are very few civil society actors that focus solely on SSG/R, they are also aware if the government is not being consistent in pursuing other reforms that accomplish similar good governance and SDGs. This unavoidably exposes governments to policy hypocrisy and can erode the trust between the government and civil society. Specifically, the government must be able to impose this reform orientation on security providers such as the military and police. While this could be a challenge given potential imbalances between civilian politicians and armed forces, this is where the government could be aided by civil society in providing legitimacy to reform efforts, despite possible resistance from security providers.

   c. *Engage in continuous and meaningful dialogue with civil society*. This paper emphasized the importance of the relationship between civil society and security providers. The case of *BB* in the Philippines showed that institutionalized mechanisms of consultation and dialogue generate trust and confidence between them. Developing mutual trust and respect is often a gradual process, but cases around the world have shown that this can be done with consistent effort and patience and adopting open minds. Communicative channels should be maintained despite possible strain in the relationship and changes in leadership.

3. For civil society

   a. *Acquire more knowledge and be updated on SSG/R*. Civil society's power is often derived from its ability to engage in advocacy that is premised on possessing the necessary knowledge and information. To this end, it must continue to equip itself with the means by which it can deal with the larger security sector. It must avoid falling into stereotypes, outdated impressions, and unbacked assumptions about the government and security institutions. It must seek opportunities to improve its stock knowledge on SSG/R, given that it is a highly evolving global discourse. To this end, it must invest in its research capabilities but also engage in projects that continuously monitor the state of SSG in the country or countries in which they operate.

   b. *Seek to clarify and institutionalize partnerships with the security sector*. Before embarking on partnerships with the security sector, civil society groups must clarify the terms of engagement as well as clarify the roles that they play in SSR processes. Collaboration on initiatives such as oversight, research and analysis, and even service delivery needs to be carefully deliberated and crafted to ensure their substantive implementation. The case of the Philippines showed that sustainability of good practices that link SSG/R with SDG-16 can be undermined by changes in political leadership. Specifically, the rise of populist-authoritarian leadership diminished the space for civil society participation in SSG, particularly its role as an informal source of civilian oversight and accountability of the security sector. Given this experience, CSOs need to develop more sustainable mechanisms of cooperation and partnership in different levels of governance and decision-making. They could also strive to maintain relations with bureaucrats and other officials not subject to electoral cycles. Institutionalization also possibly entails transforming cooperative partnerships into policies that will be difficult to be arbitrarily undermined by a new set of leaders and officials.

   c. *Integrate SSG/R with SDG implementation and vice versa*. This paper showed the significant overlap between these two discourses. CSOs advocating sustainable development could benefit from learning about SSR and including them in their advocacies. The inexorable relationship between these two discourses should be mainstreamed in the programs of civil society. Conversely, CSOs engaged in SSR need to include how their advocacy efforts could have implications for meeting SDG targets, especially in building sustainable peace, justice, and strong institutions.

   d. *Practice good governance principles*. The final policy recommendation seems like a given, but civil society must not be exempt from the demands of transparency, accountability, and participation that it seeks from other members of the security sector. Failure to do so will expose civil society with democratic deficits that could undermine its legitimacy and credibility. Therefore, it must resist the urge to be exempt from being subject to these principles. This requires much self-restraint but also consistent efforts to consult with their chosen constituencies.

CHAPTER VI

References

Africa Center for Strategic Studies. (2018). *Security sector reform in Somalia. Aims for lasting peace*. Retrieved from thenewhumanitarian.org.

Alagappa, M. (2001). *Coercion and governance: The declining political role of the military in Asia*. Stanford: Stanford University Press.

Alagappa, M. (2004). *Civil society and political change in Asia: expanding and contracting democratic space*. Palo Alto: Stanford University Press.

Amnesty International. (2007). *Tunisia: Human rights briefing for the 20th anniversary of President Ben Ali's rule*. Press Release. https://www.amnesty.org/en/latest/press-release/2007/11/tunisia-human-rights-briefing-20th-anniversary-president-ben-alie28099s-rule/.

Anheier, H. (2013). *Civil society: Measurement, evaluation, policy*. London: Routledge.

Arugay, A. A. (2008). Linking security sector reform to peacebuilding and development in the Philippines: A best practice case. *Journal of Peacebuilding & Development, 4*(2), 100–105.

Arugay, A. A. (2021). Civil society and the security sector in the Philippines after 9/11: Tensions between democracy and homeland security. In S. N. Romaniuk & E. T. Njoku (Eds.), *Counterterrorism and civil society: Post-9/11 progress and challenges* (pp. 283–294). Manchester: Manchester University Press.

Arugay, A. A. (2023). Militarizing governance: Informal civil–military relations and democratic erosion in the Philippines. In A. Chong & N. Jenne (Eds.), *Asian military evolutions: Civil–military relations in Asia* (pp. 68–89). Bristol: Bristol University Press.

Arugay, A., Batac, M., & Street, J. (2021). *An explosive cocktail: Counterterrorism, militarisation, and authoritarianism in the Philippines*. London: Saferworld.

Ansorg, N. (2017). Security sector reform in Africa: Donor approaches versus local needs. *Contemporary Security Policy, 38*(1), 129–144.

Ansorg, N., & Gordon, E. (2019). Co-operation, contestation and complexity in post-conflict security sector reform. *Journal of Intervention and Statebuilding, 13*(1), 2–24.

Baker, G. (2003). *Civil society and democratic theory: Alternative voices*. London: Routledge.

Baker, B. (2010). Linking state and non-State security and justice. *Development Policy Review, 28*(5), 597–616.

Baker, B., & Scheye, E. (2007). Multi-layered justice and security delivery in post-conflict and fragile states: Analysis. *Conflict, Security & Development, 7*(4), 503–528.

Ball, N., & Brzoska, M. (2002). *Voice and accountability in the security sector*. Bonn: Bonn International Center for Conversion.

Baranyi, S. (2019). Second-generation SSR or unending violence in Haiti?. *Stability: International Journal of Security and Development, 8*(1), 1–19.

Beeson, M, Bellamy, A. J., & Hughes, B. (2006). Taming the tigers? Reforming the security sector in Southeast Asia. *The Pacific Review, 19*(4), 449–472.

Bendix, D., & Stanley, R. (2008). Deconstructing local ownership of security sector reform: A review of the literature. *African Security Studies 17*(2), 93–104.

Bernhard, M., Fernandes, T., & Branco, R. (2017). Introduction: civil society and democracy in an era of inequality. *Comparative Politics, 49*(3), 297–309.

Bertelsmann Stiftung. (2022). BTI 2022 Country Report: Tunisia. https://bti-project.org/en/reports/country-dashboard/TUN.

Burt, G. (2016). *Security sector reform, legitimate politics, and SDG 16. SSR 2.O Brief*. Ontario: Center for Security Governance.

Bryden, A. & H. Hänggi (Eds.). (2004). *Reform and reconstruction of the security sector*. Geneva: DCAF.

Cariño, L. (2002). *Between the state and the market: The nonprofit sector and civil society in the Philippines*. Quezon City: Center for Leadership, Citizenship, and Democracy.

Carothers, T. & M. Ottaway (Eds.). 2000. *Funding virtue: Civil society aid and democracy promotion*. Washington: Carnegie Endowment for International Peace.

Carroll, T., & Jarvis, D. S. (2015). The new politics of development: Citizens, civil society, and the evolution of neoliberal development policy. *Globalizations, 12*(3), 281–304.

Catholic Relief Services. (2019). *Getting it right: Policy recommendations for preventing and countering violent extremism*. https://www.crs.org/sites/default/files/tools-research/final_cve_policy_note.pdf.

Cawthra, G. & R. Luckham, (Eds.). 2003. *Governing insecurity: Democratic control of military and security establishments in transitional democracies*. London: Zed Books.

Chaker, M. (2021). Tunisian civil society and the shrinking margin of freedom. Project on Middle East Democracy. https://pomed.org/publication/tunisian-civil-society-and-the-shrinking-margin-of-freedom/.

Chambers, P. (2014). Superficial consolidation: Security sector governance and the executive branch in the Philippines today. In F. Heiduk (Ed.), *Security sector reform in Southeast Asia: From policy to Practice* (pp. 102–130). London: Palgrave Macmillan UK.

Chanaa, J. (2002). *Security sector reform: Issues, challenges, and prospects*. Oxford: Oxford University Press.

Chikwanha, A. B. (2021). A constitutional based transformative approach to reform the security sector in Africa's post liberation war countries. *African Security Review, 30*(2), 170–183.

Chong, A. & N. Jenne (Eds.), *Asian military evolutions: Civil–military relations in Asia*. Bristol: Bristol University Press.

CIVIC. (2017a). *Empowering Afghan civil society and communities on civilian protection: Key takeaways*. London: CIVIC.

CIVIC. (2017b). *Counter-terror and the logic of violence in Somalia's civil war: Time for a new approach*. London: CIVIC.

CIVIC. (2019). *Niger: A bulwark against further instability in West Africa*. CSIS Briefs. https://www.csis.org/analysis/niger-bulwark-against-further-instability-west-africa.

CIVICUS. (2021). CIVICU Monitor. monitor.civicus.org.

CIVICUS. (2019). *Citizen generated data for SDG-16: Inclusive and responsive decision-making*. Retrieved from civicus.org.

Clarke, G. (2000). *The politics of NGOs in Southeast Asia: Participation and protest in the Philippines*. London: Routledge.

Cohen, J. L., & Arato, A. (1992). *Civil society and political theory*. Cambridge: MIT Press.

Cubitt, C. (2013). Constructing civil society: an intervention for building peace?. *Peacebuilding, 1*(1), 91–108.

Dattler, R. (2016). Not without us: civil society's role in implementing the sustainable development goals. *Entre Nous, 84,* 18–21. https://eeca.unfpa.org/sites/default/files/pub-pdf/Entre-Nous-84-full-book.pdf.

DCAF (Geneva Centre for the Democratic Control of Armed Forces). (2015). The Security Sector. SSR Backgrounder Series. Geneva: DCAF. https://www.dcaf.ch/sites/default/files/publications/documents/DCAF_BG_03_TheSecuritySector_EN_Jul2022.pdf.

DCAF (Geneva Centre for the Democratic Control of Armed Forces). (2017). *Security sector development in Tunisia: Country assessment and results monitoring.* Geneva: DCAF. https://aidstream.org/files/documents/IATI---TFNA-Tunisia-2017-20180713010724.pdf.

DCAF (Geneva Centre for Security Sector Governance). (2019). Civil Society. SSR Backgrounder Series. Geneva: DCAF. https://www.dcaf.ch/sites/default/files/publications/documents/DCAF_BG_17_CivilSociety_Nov2022.pdf.

DCAF (Geneva Centre for the Democratic Control of Armed Forces). (2020). *Linking security sector governance and reform to the sustainable development goals: An analysis of voluntary national reviews (2016–2019).* Geneva: DCAF.

de Tocqueville, A. (1969). Democracy in America. Trans. by George Lawrence. Garden City, NY: Anchor Books.

Deane, S. (2013). *Transforming Tunisia: The role of civil society in Tunisia's transition.* London: International Alert.

Detzner, S. (2017). Modern post-conflict security sector reform in Africa: Patterns of success and failure. *African Security Review, 26*(2), 116–142.

Diamond, L., &. Plattner, M. F. (Eds.) (1996). *Civil-military relations and democracy.* Baltimore: Johns Hopkins University Press.

Donais, T. (2018). Security sector reform and the challenge of vertical integration. *Journal of Intervention and Statebuilding, 12*(1), 31–47.

Dryzek, J. S. (2012). *Foundations and frontiers of deliberative governance.* Oxford: Oxford University Press.

Dursun-Özkanca, O. (2021). *The nexus between security sector governance/reform and Sustainable Development Goal-16: An examination of conceptual linkages and policy recommendations.* London: Ubiquity Press. DOI: https://doi.org/10.5334/bcm.

Ebo, A. (2007). The role of security sector reform in sustainable development: Donor policy trends and challenges. *Conflict, Security & Development, 7*(1), 27–60.

Edmunds, T. (2004). Security sector reform: Concepts and implementation. In P. Fluri, & M. Hadzic (Eds.), *Sourcebook on security sector reform.* Geneva: DCAF.

Edwards, M. (2009). *Civil society.* Cambridge: Polity Press.

Edwards, B., & Foley, M. W. (1998). Beyond Tocqueville: Civil society and social capital in comparative perspective. *American Behavioral Scientist, 42*(1), 5–20.

Eickhoff, K. (2021). Navigating ownership in the context of the security sector reform (SSR) in Mali: A comparison of external actors' approaches. *Journal of Intervention and Statebuilding, 15*(3), 386–405.

El Baradei, L. (2020). Politics of evidence based policy making: Reporting on SDG 16 in Egypt. *International Journal of Public Administration, 43*(5), 425–440.

Felbab-Brown, V. (2018). The hard, hot, dusty road to accountability, reconciliation, and peace in Somalia. Washington DC: Brookings Institution. https://www.brookings.edu/articles/the-hard-hot-dusty-road-to-accountability-reconciliation-and-peace-in-somalia/.

Fischer, M. & B. Schmelzle (Eds.). (2009). *Building peace in the absence of states: Challenging the discourse on state failure.* Berlin: Berghof Research Center for Constructive Conflict Management.

Fitz-Gerald, A. (2003). Security sector reform: Streamlining national military forces to respond to the wider security needs. *Journal of Security Sector Management, 1*(1), 1–21.

Fluri, P. & M. Hadzic (Eds.). (2006). *Sourcebook on security sector reform.* Geneva: DCA

Fluri, P. & F. Molnar (Eds.). (2006). *Civil society and the security sector: Concepts and practices in new democracies.* Geneva: DCAF.

Forman, J. (2006). Civil society, democracy and the law. In M. Caparini, P. Fluri, & F. Molnar (Eds.), *Civil society and the security sector: Concepts and practices in new democracies.* Geneva: DCAF.

FORUS et al. (2019). *Realizing the potential of goal 15 of the 2030 Agenda to promote and protect civic space.* Retrieved from unescap.org.

Freedom House. (2022). *Freedom in the world 2022.* https://freedomhouse.org/sites/default/files /2022-02/FIW_2022_PDF_Booklet_Digital_Final_Web.pdf.

Gellner, E. (1994). Nationalisms and the new world order. *Bulletin of the American Academy of Arts and Sciences, 47*(5), 29–36.

Ghimire, S. (2019). *The politics of peacebuilding: Emerging actors and security sector reform in conflict-affected states.* New York: Routledge.

Ginifer, J. (2006). The challenge of the security sector and security reform processes in democratic transitions: The case of Sierra Leone. *Democratization 13*(5).

Gluck, J., & Brandt, M. (2015). *Participatory and inclusive constitution-making: Giving voice to the demands of citizens in the wake of the Arab Spring.* Washington, DC: United States Institute of Peace.

Gordon, E. (2014). Security sector reform, statebuilding and local ownership: Securing the state or its people? *Journal of Intervention and Statebuilding, 8*(2–3), 126–148.

Greene, O. (2003). Security sector reform, conflict prevention and regional perspectives. *Journal of Security Sector Management, 1*(1), 1–15.

Greitens, S. C. (2016). *Dictators and their secret police: Coercive institutions and state violence.* Cambridge: Cambridge University Press.

Grugel, J. (2003). Democratization studies: citizenship, globalization and governance. *Government and Opposition, 38*(2), 238–264.

Hänggi, H. (2003). Making sense of security sector governance. In H. Hänggi, & T. H. Winkler (Eds.), *Challenges of security sector governance* (pp. 1–22). Geneva: DCAF.

Hänggi, H. (2004). Conceptualizing security sector reform and reconstruction. In A. Bryden, & H. Hänggi (Eds.), *Reform and reconstruction of the security sector* (pp. 3–20). Geneva: DCAF.

Hänggi, H. & T. H. Winkler (Eds.). (2003). *Challenges of security sector governance.* Geneva: DCAF. Haugbølle, R., & Chemlali, A. (2019). *Everyday violence and security in Tunisia.* https://www .mei.edu/publications/everyday-violence-and-security-tunisia#:~:text=The%20repression %20and%20the%20everyday,as%20a%20premise%20of%20life. Hayes, C. J. (2017). *Nations in Transit-2001–2002: Civil Society, Democracy and Markets in East Central Europe and Newly Independent States.* Routledge.

Heiduk, F. (Ed). (2016). *Security sector reform in Southeast Asia: From policy to practice.* Basingstoke: Palgrave Macmillan.

Henderson, S. L. (2011). Civil society in Russia: State-society relations in the post-Yeltsin era. *Problems of Post-Communism, 58*(3), 11–27.

Homel, P., & Nasson, N. (2016). Partnerships for human security in fragile contexts: Where community safety and security sector reform intersect. *Australian Journal of International Affairs, 70*(3), 311–327.

Human Development Network. (2005). *Philippine human development report: Peace, human security and human development in the Philippines.* Manila: HDN.

Human Rights Watch. (2011). *Tunisia's repressive laws: The reform agenda.* New York: Human Rights Watch. https://www.hrw.org/report/2011/12/16/tunisias-repressive-laws/reform-agenda.

Human Rights Watch. (2021). Somalia: Events of 2021. In *World Report 2022: Events of 2021*. New York: Human Rights Watch.

Huntington, S. P. (1968). Political order in changing societies New Haven: Yale University Press.

Huntington, S. P. (1993). *The third wave: Democratization in the late twentieth century*. Norman: University of Oklahoma Press.

Ibezim-Ohaeri, V. (n.d.). *FATF and civic space: Lessons from Nigeria*. Retrieved from FATF and Civic Space: Lessons from Nigeria – Closing Spaces.

ICAN. (2017a). *Preventing violent extremism, protecting rights, and community policing: Why civil society and security sector partnership matter*. Retrieved from icanpeacework.org.

ICAN. (2017b). *From the ground up: A preliminary dialogue on the nexus of economic policy, gender, and violent extremism*. Retrieved from icanpeacework.org.

Institute for Economic and Peace. (2016). Global Peace Index 2016. https://www.visionofhumanity .org/wp-content/uploads/2020/10/GPI-2016-Report_2.pdf.

Ivanovic, A., Cooper, H., & Nguyen, A. M. (2018). Institutionalisation of SDG 16: More a trickle than a cascade?. *Social Alternatives, 37*(1), 49–57.

Jackson, P. (2018). Introduction: Second-generation security sector reform. *Journal of Intervention and Statebuilding, 12*(1), 1–10.

Kaldor, M. (2003). The idea of global civil society. *International Affairs, 79*(3), 583–593.

Kartas, M. (2014). Foreign aid and security sector reform in Tunisia: Resistance and autonomy of the security forces. *Mediterranean Politics, 19*(3), 373–391.

Kaltenborn, M., M. Krajewski, & H. Kuhn (Eds.). (2020). *Sustainable Development Goals and Human Rights* (pp. 155–169). Springer International Publishing.

Keane, J. (1998). *Civil society: Old images, new visions*. Cambridge: Polity Press.

Keck, M. E., & Sikkink, K. (1998). *Activists beyond borders: Advocacy networks in international politics*. Ithaca: Cornell University Press.

Kempe, R. H. S. (2020). Peace, justice and inclusive institutions: overcoming challenges to the implementation of Sustainable Development Goal 16, *Global Change, Peace & Security, 32*(1), 57–77, DOI: https://doi.org/10.1080/14781158.2019.1667320.

Koplow, M. (2011). Why Tunisia's revolution is Islamist-free. *Foreign Policy*. https://foreignpolicy .com/2011/01/14/why-tunisias-revolution-is-islamist-free-2/.

Krause, K., & Jutersonke, O. (2005). Peace, security and development in post-conflict environments. *Security Dialogue, 36*(4), 447–62.

Laberge, M., & Touihri, N. (2019). Can SDG-16 data drive national accountability? A cautiously optimistic view. *Global Policy, 10*(51), 153–156.

Lang, S. (2012). *NGOs, civil society, and the public sphere*. Cambridge: Cambridge University Press.

Lazarus, L. (2020). Securitizing sustainable development? The coercive sting in SDG 16. In M. Kaltenborn, M. Krajewski, & H. Kuhn (Eds.), *Sustainable Development Goals and Human Rights* (pp. 155–169). Springer International Publishing.

Lederlach, J. P., Clos, R., Ansel, D., Greene, A. L., Weis, L., Brandwein, J., & Lee, S. (2011). Somalia: Creating space for fresh approaches to peacebuilding. Uppsala: Life & Peace Institute. https:// africaportal.org/publication/somalia-creating-space-fresh-approaches-peacebuilding/.

Life & Peace Institute. (2014). Alternatives for conflict transformation in Somalia: A snapshot and analysis of key political actors' views and strategies. Uppsala: Life & Peace Institute. https:// life-peace.org/resource/alternatives-for-conflict-transformation-in-somalia/.

Linke, J. (2020). Provisions on SSR and DDR in Peace Agreements. SSR Thematic Brief: Geneva: Geneva Centre for Security Sector Governance (DCAF). https://www.dcaf.ch/sites/default /files/publications/documents/EN_SSR_DDR_Peace_Agreements_2020.pdf.

Loada, A., & Moderan, O. (2015). Civil society involvement in security sector reform and governance. Geneva: DCAF. https://www.dcaf.ch/sites/default/files/publications/documents/ECOWAS _Toolkit_T6_EN.pdf.

Loden, A. (2007). Civil society and security sector reform in post-conflict Liberia: Painting a moving train without brushes. *The International Journal of Transitional Justice, 1*(2), 297–307.

Lottholz, P. (2020). *The roles and practices of civil society actors in police reform in Kyrgyzstan: Activism, expertise, knowledge production.* International Peacekeeping, 28(1), 52–83. DOI: https://doi.org/10.1080/13533312.2020.1792296.

Luckham, R. (2003). Democratic strategies for security in transition and conflict. In G. Cawthra & R. Luckham, (Eds.), *Governing insecurity: Democratic control of military and security establishments in transitional democracies* (pp. 3–28). London: Zed Books.

Malik, S. (2009). Security sector reforms in Pakistan: Challenges, remedies, and future prospects. *South Asian Survey, 16*(2), 273–289.

McFaul, M. (2002). The fourth wave of democracy and dictatorship: noncooperative transitions in the postcommunist world. *World politics, 54*(2), 212–244.

Menkhaus, K. (2016). Non-state security providers and political formation in Somalia. *CSG Papers.* Center for Security Governance. https://reliefweb.int/report/somalia/non-state -security-providers-and-political-formation-somalia.

Mnasri, A. (2016). *Enabling environment national assessment of civil society in Tunisia.* Amman: Kawakibi Democratic Transition Center. https://www.civicus.org/index.php/eena-country /tunisia.

Nathan, L. (2007). *No ownership, no commitment: A guide to local ownership of security sector reform.* Birmingham: GFN-SSR.

Nygård, H. M. (2017). Achieving the sustainable development agenda: The governance–conflict nexus. *International Area Studies Review, 20*(1), 3–18.

NYU Paris Public Interest Clinic. (2021). *Bank de-risking of non-profit clients: A business and human rights perspective.* Paris: New York University.

O'Donnell, G. A., Schmitter, P. C., & Whitehead, L. (Eds.). (1986). *Transitions from authoritarian rule: Southern Europe.* Baltimore: Johns Hopkins University Press.

OECD (Organization for Economic Cooperation and Development). (2005). *Security System Reform and Governance A DAC Reference Document.* Paris: OECD Publishing. https://www .oecd-ilibrary.org/security-system-reform-and-governance_5lmkl60tv5q5.pdf.

Official Gazette of the Republic of the Philippines. (2012). OPAPP lauds reforms in the PHL security sector. https://www.officialgazette.gov.ph/2012/03/12/opapp-lauds-reforms-in-the-phl -security-sector/.

Osman, F. (2018). The role of civil society in Somalia's reconstruction: achievements, challenges and opportunities. https://www.saferworld-global.org/resources/news-and-analysis /post/775-the-role-of-civil-society-in-somaliaas-reconstruction-achievements-challenges -and-opportunities#:~:text=Somali%20civil%20society%20has%20an,bridges%20in%20a %20polarised%20society.

Racelis, M. (2000). New visions and strong actions: Civil society in the Philippines. In T. Carothers, & M. Ottaway (Eds.), *Funding virtue: Civil society aid and democracy promotion* (pp. 159–187). Washington: Carnegie Endowment for International Peace.

Ramcharan, R. (2021). SDG 16 and the human rights architecture in Southeast Asia: A complementary protection process. *Journal of Human Rights, 20*(2), 228–244.

Rauch, J. (2011). Civil society and security sector oversight. *African Security Review, 20*(4), 21–33.

Reyes, C. M., Albert, J., Ramon, G., Tabuga, A. D., Arboneda, A. A., Vizmanos, J. F. V., & Cabaero, C. C. (2019). *The Philippines' voluntary national review on the sustainable development goals.* Philippine Institute for Development Studies. http://hdl.handle.net/11540/11359.

Robbins, M. (2015). After the Arab Spring: People still want democracy. *Journal of Democracy 26*(4), 80–89.

Romaniuk, S. N. & E. T. Njoku (Eds.), *Counter-terrorism and civil society: Post-9/11 progress and challenges.* Manchester: Manchester University Press.

Roht-Arriaza, N. (2022). Civil society in processes of accountability. In M. Cherif Bassiouni (Ed.), *Post-Conflict Justice* (pp. 97–114). Leiden: Brill.

Saferworld. (2016). *Barbed wires on our heads: Lessons from counter-terror, stabilization, and state-building in Somalia.* London: Saferworld.

Saferworld. (2019). *A threat inflated? The countering and preventing violent extremism agenda in Kyrgyzstan.* London: Saferworld.

Scarpello, F. (2014). Stifled development: The SSR — Civil society organizations community in post-authoritarian Indonesia. In F. Heiduk (Ed.), *Security sector reform in Southeast Asia: From policy to practice* (pp. 131–158). London: Palgrave Macmillan.

Schmeidl, S. (2009). 'Prêt-a-porter states': How the McDonaldization of state-building misses the mark in Afghanistan. In M. Fischer, & B. Schmelzle (Eds.), *Building peace in the absence of states: Challenging the discourse on state failure* (pp. 67–78). Berlin: Berghof Research Center for Constructive Conflict Management.

Schirch, L. & D. Mancini-Griffoli. (2015). *Local ownership in Security: Case studies of peacebuilding approaches.* The Hague: Alliance for Peacebuilding. https://gppac.net/files/2019-01/Local%20 Ownership%20in%20Security%20Report.%2015%20March%202016.pdf.

Scholte, J. A. (2011). Towards greater legitimacy in global governance. *Review of International Political Economy, 18*(1), 110–120.

Schroeder, U., Chappuis, F. & Kocak, D. (2014). Security sector reform and the emergence of hybrid security governance. *International Peacekeeping 21*(2), 214–230.

Sedra, M. (2010). Towards second generation security sector reform. In M. Sedra (Ed.), *The future of security sector reform.* Waterloo: Center for International Governance Innovation.

Sénit, C. A. (2020). Leaving no one behind? The influence of civil society participation on the Sustainable Development Goals. *Environment and Planning C: Politics and Space, 38*(4), 693–712.

Shah, H., & Dalton, M. (2020). *The evolution of Tunisia's military and the role of foreign security sector assistance.* Working paper. Carnegie Middle East Center. https://carnegie-mec.org/2020/04/29 /evolution-of-tunisia-s-military-and-role-of-foreign-security-sector-assistance-pub-81602.

SOLIDAR. (n.d.). *Economic and social rights report: El Salvador zoom on shrinking space for civil society.* https://www.solidar.org/system/downloads/attachments/000/001/242/original/Solidar -El-Salvador-v06.pdf?1612953468.

Somali Institute for Development Research and Analysis. (2019). The Role Of Civil Society Organizations In SDGs Localization In Somalia. https://sidrainstitute.org/publications/the -role-of-civil-society-organizations-in-sdgs-localization-in-somalia/.

Sombatpoonsiri, J. (2018). Securing peace? Regime types and security sector reform in the Patani (Thailand) and Bangsamoro (the Philippines) peace processes, 2011–2016. *Strategic Analysis, 42*(4), 377–401.

Stepan, A., & Linz, J. (2013). Democratization theory and the Arab Spring. *Journal of Democracy, 24*(2), 15–30.

Sunil, S. (2016). "Barbed wire on our heads": Lessons from counter-terror, stabilization and state-building in Somalia. London: Saferworld. https://www.files.ethz.ch/isn/195878/barbed-wire -on-our-heads.pdf.

Tarrow, S. (2005). *The new transnational activism.* Cambridge University Press.

Thompson, M. R. (1995). *The anti-Marcos struggle: Personalistic rule and democratic transition in the Philippines.* New Haven: Yale University Press.

Torres, L. (2021). *A civil or uncivil civil society?* New York: Center on International Cooperation.

Transparency International. (2020). Government Defense Integrity Index. ti-defence.org/gdi.

Tyner, J. A. (2005). *Iraq, terror, and the Philippines' will to war.* Lanham: Rowman & Littlefield.

Uddin, M. (2009). Security sector reform in Bangladesh. *South Asian Survey, 16*(2), 209–230.

UN Assistance Mission in Somalia. (2017). Protection of Civilians: Building the Foundation for Peace, Security and Human Rights in Somalia. *Country Report.* https://www.ohchr.org/en

/documents/country-reports/protection-civilians-building-foundation-peace-security-and
-human-rights.

United Nations. (2013). Sustainable Development Goals. un.org/sustainabledevelopment/peace
-justice.

United Nations. (2022). Sustainable Development Report. un.org/sustainabledevelopment/progress
-report.

United Nations Secretary-General. (2013, August 13). *Report of the Secretary-General. Securing
states and societies: Strengthening the United Nations comprehensive support to security sector
reform.* A/67/970 S/2013/480. https://digitallibrary.un.org/record/619044/files/A_62_659
%26S_2008_39-EN.pdf?ln=en.

US Department of State. (2009, April 30). *Country reports on terrorism 2008 – Tunisia.* Retrieved
from http://www.state.gov/s/ct/rls/crt/2008/122433.htm.

Wardak, M., Zaman, I., & Nawabi, K. (2007). The role and functions of religious civil society in
Afghanistan: Case studies from Sayedabad & Kunduz. Kabul: Cooperation for Peace and Unity
(CPAU).

White, G. (2004). Civil society, democratization and development: Clearing the analytical ground.
In P. Burnell & P. Calver (Eds.), *Civil society in democratization.* London: Frank Cass & Co.

World Bank. (2020). *Somalia economic update. Impact of COVID-19: Policies to manage the crisis
and strengthen economic recovery.* Washington DC: The World Bank.

Wulf, H. (2011). Security sector reform in developing and transitional countries revisited. https://
berghof-foundation.org/files/publications/wulf_handbookII.pdf.

Zamfir, I. (2020). *Peace, justice, and strong institutions: EU support for implementing SDG 16 worldwide.* Strasbourg: European Parliamentary Research Service. https://www.europarl.europa.eu
/RegData/etudes/BRIE/2020/646156/EPRS_BRI(2020)646156_EN.pdf.

1 *There are many ways of completing this question. Either of the specimen completions below would receive full marks.*   (15)

EITHER

(a) *Chords are shown here with roman numerals AND notes on the stave. EITHER of these methods of notation would receive full marks. Other recognised methods of notation will also be considered and marks awarded accordingly.*

Ia   viia   Va   Ib   iia   Va   iiib   viia   iib   Ib   IVa   Ic   Va   Ia

OR

(b)

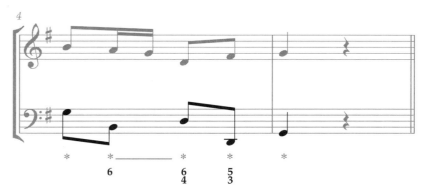

2 *There are many ways of completing this question. The specimen completion below would receive full marks.* (15)

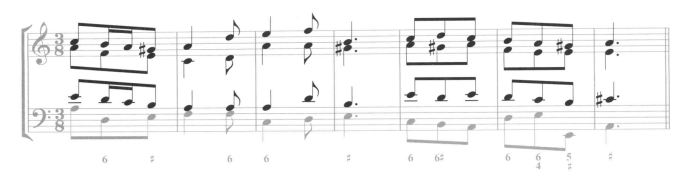

3 *There are many ways of completing this question. Either of the specimen completions below would receive full marks.* (20)
The given openings are printed in grey in order to distinguish them from the completion, but candidates must include the opening in their answer.

EITHER

(a) *Source: Mendelssohn, Intermezzo from 'A Midsummer Night's Dream', Op. 61 No. 9*

bassoon

OR

(b) trumpet

4 *Source: Mendelssohn, Songs Without Words, Op. 67 No. 5*

   (a) Bar 2   V⁷d / V⁷d major   (3)

           Bar 3   ii°b / IIb diminished   (3)

   (b) (i)   7–8   (2)

        (ii) 8–9   (2)

        (iii) 16   (2)

        (iv) 14   (2)

        (v) 8   (2)

   (c) Similarity   melody / rhythm of top line / harmony   (1)

        One mark will be awarded (up to a maximum of three marks) for each correct reference to the following: (3)

        Differences   articulation / 'a tempo' in bar 18 / dynamics / fuller chords used in bars 22–23

   (d) X   unaccented passing note   (2)

        Y   note of anticipation   (2)

   (e)   Mendelssohn   (1)

5 (a) roll / drum roll / rapid reiteration of the same note   (2)

        plucked / pluck the strings   (2)

        divided / divided into two parts   (2)

   (b) (i)   Clarinet   (2)

        (ii) Horns   (2)

   (c) (i)   violas; first violins; second oboe   (3)

        (ii) piccolo   (2)

   (d) 1   perfect 12th / compound perfect 5th   (2)

        2   major 6th   (2)

        3   diminished 5th   (2)

   (e) (i)   false   (2)

        (ii) false   (2)

Theory Paper   Grade 6   2019   B
Model Answers

1 *There are many ways of completing this question. Either of the specimen completions below would receive full marks.*   (15)

EITHER

(a) *Chords are shown here with roman numerals AND notes on the stave. EITHER of these methods of notation would receive full marks. Other recognised methods of notation will also be considered and marks awarded accordingly.*

OR

(b)   **Affettuoso**

2 *There are many ways of completing this question. The specimen completion below would receive full marks.* (15)

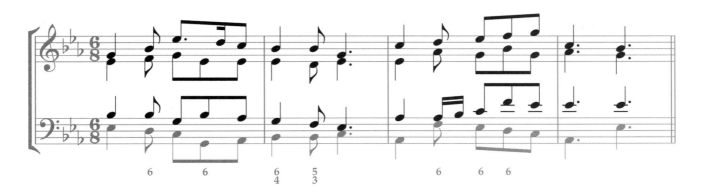

3 *There are many ways of completing this question. Either of the specimen completions below would receive full marks.* (20) *The given openings are printed in grey in order to distinguish them from the completion, but candidates must include the opening in their answer.*

EITHER

(a) *Source: MacDowell, From a German Forest, from 'Fireside Tales', Op. 61*

cello

OR

(b) flute

4 *Source: Haydn, Verzweiflung (Despair)*

(a) *All possible answers are shown on the extract reproduced below. For full marks, candidates need to identify only one example of each answer.*

B Bar 14 (2)

C Bar 9 (2)

D Bar 10 / 16 (2)

(b)

(3)

(c) Bar 3   ii⁷b / II⁷b minor / IV⁶a / IV⁶a major (3)

Bar 4   V⁷c / V⁷c major (3)

(d) (i) true (2)

(ii) false (2)

(e) X   grace notes (2)

Y   accented passing note / appoggiatura / leaning note (2)

Z   upper auxiliary note (2)

5

(a) getting slower / gradually getting slower (2)

calm / tranquil (2)

roll / drum roll / rapid reiteration of the same note (2)

(b) (i) violas; first horn (2)

(ii) timpani; second horn (2)

(iii) B♭ (2)

(c) (i) Horns 1/2

(2)

(ii) Clarinet

(3)

(d) *One mark will be awarded (up to a maximum of two marks) for each correct reference to the following:* (2)
use of accents and tenuto / louder dynamic marking / highest sounding instrument /
espress. and hairpins / reduced orchestration

(e) Bassoon 1

(2)

(f) (i) false (2)

(ii) false (2)

Theory Paper   Grade 6   2019   C
Model Answers

1 *There are many ways of completing this question. Either of the specimen completions below would receive full marks.*   (15)

EITHER

(a) *Chords are shown here with roman numerals AND notes on the stave. EITHER of these methods of notation would receive full marks. Other recognised methods of notation will also be considered and marks awarded accordingly.*

OR

(b) **Tempo moderato**

2 *There are many ways of completing this question. The specimen completion below would receive full marks.* (15)

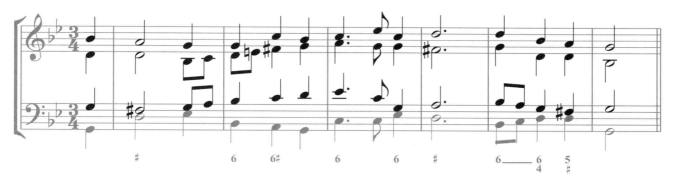

3 *There are many ways of completing this question. Either of the specimen completions below would receive full marks.* (20) *The given openings are printed in grey in order to distinguish them from the completion, but candidates must include the opening in their answer.*

EITHER

(a) *Source: Haydn, String Quartet in E flat, Op. 33 No. 2, last movement*

flute

OR

(b) clarinet

4 *Source: Melartin, Sad Moments, Op. 9 No. 5*

   (a) simple / plain (2)

       broadening / getting a little slower (2)

   (b) Bar 4   V^{7}c / V^{7}c major (3)

       Bar 15   ii$^{\circ 7}$b / II^{7}b diminished / iv^{6}a / IV^{6}a minor (3)

   (c) (i) 4 (2)

       (ii) 3 / 11 (2)

       (iii) 3 (2)

       (iv) 6 (2)

   (d) *One mark will be awarded (up to a maximum of three marks) for each correct reference to the following:* (3)

     allargando / pause mark / use of spread chords in bars 8–10 / descending bass line / crescendo leading to $\boldsymbol{f}$ in bar 9

   (e) (i) false (2)

       (ii) true (2)

5 (a) stopped / hand-stopped (2)

       hurrying a little (4)

   (b) (i)   (3)

       (ii)   (2)

   (c) (i)   first violins; cor anglais (2)

       (ii)   double basses; second bassoon (2)

       (iii) 5 (2)

   (d) **1** diminished 5th (2)

      2 major 2nd (2)

      3 minor 6th (2)

   (e) false (2)

Theory Paper Grade 6 2019 S
Model Answers

1 *There are many ways of completing this question. Either of the specimen completions below would receive full marks.* (15)

EITHER

(a) *Chords are shown here with roman numerals AND notes on the stave. EITHER of these methods of notation would receive full marks. Other recognised methods of notation will also be considered and marks awarded accordingly.*

OR

(b)

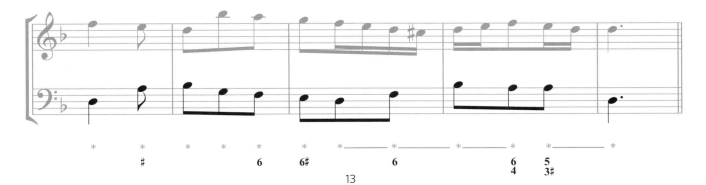

2 *There are many ways of completing this question. The specimen completion below would receive full marks.* (15)

3 *There are many ways of completing this question. Either of the specimen completions below would receive full marks.* (20) *The given openings are printed in grey in order to distinguish them from the completion, but candidates must include the opening in their answer.*

EITHER

(a) *Source: Haydn, String Trio, Hob. V/3*

violin

OR

(b) bassoon

4 (a) (i) 6–8 / 7–8   (2)

    (ii) 19   (2)

    (iii) 6 / 20   (2)

(b) Bar 9 ii^7a / II^7a minor / IV^6d / IV^6d major   (3)

    Bar 15 V^7d / V^7d major   (3)

(c) X   changing note   (2)

    Y   accented passing note / appoggiatura / leaning note   (2)

    Z   lower auxiliary note   (2)

(d)   (3)

(e) (i) true   (2)

    (ii) true   (2)

5 *Source: Debussy, Fêtes from 'Nocturnes'*

(a) held back / slower   (2)

    sweet / soft   (2)

    divided / divided into two parts   (2)

    mutes / with mutes / muted   (2)

(b) (i) Horns $\frac{1}{2}$ (2)

    (ii) Clarinets in B♭ (at concert pitch)   (3)

(c) (i) side drum / snare drum   (2)

    (ii) double basses; tuba   (2)

(d) (i) true   (2)

    (ii) true   (2)

(e) 1   major 6th   (2)

    2   minor 9th / compound minor 2nd   (2)

Music Theory Practice Papers 2019 Model Answers

Model answers for four practice papers from ABRSM's 2019 Theory exams for Grade 6

Key features:

- a list of correct answers where appropriate
- a selection of likely options where the answer can be expressed in a variety of ways
- a single exemplar where a composition-style answer is required

Support material for ABRSM Music Theory exams

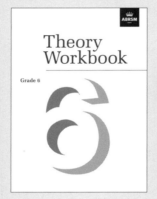

**Supporting the teaching and learning of music
in partnership with four Royal Schools of Music**

Royal Academy of Music | Royal College of Music
Royal Northern College of Music | Royal Conservatoire of Scotland

www.abrsm.org f facebook.com/abrsm
@abrsm ABRSM YouTube

ISBN 978-1-78601-378-1